CN01497234

The Sixth Handshake

A factual thriller about coincidence

What is the Sixth Handshake?

*'Six degrees of separation is the idea that **all people are six or fewer social connections away from each other**. As a result, a chain of "friend of a friend" statements can be made to connect any two people in a maximum of six steps. It is also known as the six handshakes rule.'*

Siam changed its name to Thailand in 1939.

Thank you to Peter and Dorothy for giving me life.

The First
Handshake

1998. Koh Samui. Room No. 22

In one hundred years from now somebody else will own my house, sit where I sit and own what survives of my possessions – if I'm lucky I might be remembered too.

Senior Nurse Sawa was routinely patrolling her wards and tired after a busy night. Walking alone through the dimly lit corridors, paying attention to nothing in particular, drifting off into deep random thoughts in-between checking on individual patients.

I wonder who these people are? Desperate people. People hoping to last longer on this planet, irrespective of quality. People hoping to add a few more chapters to their book of life.

God forbid if I've shortened any lives through a mistake...changed their book by shortening it. I guess in reality I'm adding chapters for these people... funny how we're all born knowing the ending of our book, death, yet we have no idea what the book is going to be about or how long it's going to last.

She shook her head at the thought and peered through another ward door with patients, who were either asleep or staring motionless at the ceiling.

I wonder how many chapters in my book? It would be interesting if I knew when my last day will be. Bet I'd do things differently. I wonder what the last word will be that passes my lips? My last thoughts? Perhaps...

Then she stopped suddenly.

She instinctively felt something wasn't right about the door behind her. She retraced her steps, still holding the coffee she had collected moments earlier, and stood outside Room Number 22. Sawa stared at the door with its fireproof glass window, a door she knew well. She rubbed her shoulder and had a premonition that something in there was going to change her life - the beginning of an unforeseen chapter in *her* life.

She knew that if she walked on, nothing would happen and that somebody else would 'take the baton' and have *their* life changed instead. She hesitated to wonder whether it be for better or for worse, should she intervene. Feeling the answer to be bad, like a moth to a flame, she inexplicably turned her body to face the door. She brought her hand up to her face to shield the outside glare and peered through the 'forbidden' window.

What Sawa saw startled her, two unconscious people lying motionless in separate beds. What Sawa didn't understand was how on earth they got there, as only minutes before, on her way to get the coffee, she'd seen *no one* in the room. Stranger still, the two people now in occupation looked as if they had been there for quite a while. She broke off her stare and questioned her judgement about what had just happened and decided to seek counsel from other staff before going in. Maybe they would know something about these people.

Nurse Sawa was stationed at Nathon Hospital, Koh Samui, which stood in isolation behind a deserted pristine white sandy beach, with its only means of access being via a narrow road through the dense jungle that lay behind. At the end of the jungle road sat an ancient wooden village where children played barefoot in the heat outside.

Further down the road towards Chaweng the jungle thinned out and was replaced by an old palm tree plantation which stopped at the tourist port of Nathon. Here a freelance Detective called Gunn worked from a police station located at its centre.

The events unfolding at the nearby hospital were also about to draw Gunn in, and inadvertently confirm his intricate understanding of the powers of coincidence, which he realised to be perpetual. He was never surprised by what life threw at him and was ready for any new directions to be forced upon him by unrelated events that didn't adhere to the boundaries of time and distance.

***

Nurse Sawa needed to know where the people in Room 22 came from and went out of the ward into the sterile foyer where a night nurse sat at a circular desk. Her shift was over too, and she was getting ready to leave. Nurse Sawa interrupted the night nurse's closing up routine and explained the situation - the night nurse reluctantly checked around for files on the couple but found nothing. She shook her head negatively and wasn't really interested anyway as it had been a long night for her.

Realising this lack of focus, Nurse Sawa went to find the ward's doctor, who she found in the canteen downstairs. He too shook his head at the question she asked, but duty-bound, left his coffee and colleagues, and led the way to Room No. 22, with Nurse Sawa following close behind. He stood silently, looking through the glass as the nurse had done thirty minutes before. He turned to her and raised his eyebrows in a quizzical way.

"When did they arrive?" he asked in his French accent.

"That's my problem... I don't know. I thought you might."

"Nope. Ok, let's go in," and the doctor pushed the door open for them to enter whilst looking at the nurse's clipboard, which he had commandeered earlier. He turned a few pages and said, "Nothing!"

"I know," said Nurse Sawa.

The doctor returned the clipboard to the nurse, put his hands in his lab coat pockets, and pondered the strange situation. *Who were these people and when did they come in... and for what?*

He pulled the covering sheet back to expose a man. He thought him to be European, in his mid to late thirties and judging by his hands, probably of a middle-class background. He was surprised to see slash marks on the man's chest, arm, and lower abdomen. The wounds had since healed and had been badly attended to at some period with stitches still intact, oddly, they had never been taken out. Odder still, thought the doctor, they were at least a year old. So *why* were they never taken out?

Many questions ran through the doctor's mind. "Have you seen these people before, I mean do you think these wounds were tended here?" he asked. Sawa shrugged her shoulders. Realising the questions to be unanswerable, as the lesions were ancient in medical timelines, he continued the questions in his mind. The nurse remained silent.

He surmised the immediate state of the patient to be comfortable after doing a few basic tests. He then turned his attention to the girl. The nurse pulled back the sheet from the girl's naked body. What was immediately noticeable, which made the normally unimpressed nurse jump, were the past stab wounds (not slash) – of which there were many. Once again, they had been stitched in the distant past. The doctor stood upright, very confused, blinked his eyes and breathed out. "Cover them and come with me," he said to the nurse, and she obeyed.

"They seem fine although in a coma – stable anyway," he said loudly, trying to relay confidence and understanding. The nurse nodded as they rushed through the unloved grey and white corridors, finally stopping at a very important looking door. The doctor knocked.

"Come in."

1998. No answers

Nurse Sawa and the doctor entered and stood quietly, until the Doctor, sitting behind an impressive desk littered with reports, gestured that they should sit. He finished writing then put his pen down and sat back in his large black chair.

His attention was immediately caught by the doctor's story – occasionally confirmed by the nurse.

The doctor nodded in affirmation and said, "Right, let me make some calls".

"Yes, Doctor Smith," replied the doctor, and calls were made.

The phone sat in its cradle for a moment whilst they all sat in awkward silence. Then the phone rang and was promptly answered by Doctor Smith. After a brief conversation he replaced the receiver and once again sat back. "No idea!" he said and stood up.

"Shall we go?" he asked calmly.

They left his office and returned to Room No. 22 where a small group of doctors had since gathered outside. Some nurses hovered in the background wondering what the all the fuss was about. When Doctor Smith arrived, the doctors stood back with respect, and he made his way into the room whilst they remained outside. He beckoned Nurse Sawa to come in and explain the series of events.

After the inconclusive inquiry, Doctor Smith decided upon a more formal meeting in the boardroom upstairs.

The doctors sat around an oval table with Doctor Smith at the head, leading the enquiry. He got up to gather his thoughts and looked out the window, where the darkening skies readied for the predictable 5 o'clock storm. People scurried around below in anticipation of the coming deluge. Doctor Smith turned around, "Any ideas?"

No ideas came from the meeting.

They decided to return to Room 22. Doctor Smith, now a little frustrated, probed and prodded the couple on their beds, whilst other doctors checked reflexes and took blood samples.

"Nothing wrong with these two but for some reason they're in a coma. Never seen or heard anything like it before. As for these stitches, ditto. Will someone get them out by the way, they're disgusting," said Doctor Smith, stroking his full white beard.

He took off his glasses and put them in his pocket when he noticed `"the unconscious man had a clenched fist. He put on his glasses again and stooped down to look a little closer. "He's holding something," Doctor Smith said out loud. The others looked down.

Nurse Sawa, who seemed to be adopted for this case by Doctor Smith, tried to unclench the man's fist and stepped back when a key fell out. One doctor gasped. Nurse Sawa picked it up and gave it to

Doctor Smith. The key had a label on it *Siam Bank* was imprinted on the tag attached to the key.

Doctor Smith left the scene and returned to his office with Nurse Sawa, who he found bright, and her attractiveness hadn't gone unnoticed. He also noted her eye for detail and presumed her to be very meticulous. "I want you to check out the key. Can you go and visit the bank please?"

Sawa liked the doctor's calm yet authoritative and polite manner – similar, she thought, to his son, who was also a doctor in the Emergency wing.

"Yes, Doctor," she replied, at the strange non-medical request, and left, closing the door gently behind her.

Doctor Smith watched her go, he then leant forward and clicked on his intercom to get his secretary. "Can you call a Detective Gunn from the local police station?"

The secretary paused briefly. "No problem, one moment."

1998. Siam Bank

Sawa drove across the island for about forty minutes to a T-shaped junction at the beginning of Chaweng High Street. She parked her car outside the Siam Bank; the phone number on the tab had led her to this particular branch, a branch she knew. A green background with red writing was the bank's trademark logo above the shop and she saw that the interior was relatively free of customers.

Sawa explained the circumstances to the receptionist who was an old friend and asked to see the manager, whereby she was requested to take a seat, which she did.

A short while later a very friendly-looking woman came out and shook her hand, asking her to come into the back office. "I am the manager," said Ming, who was roughly the same age of Sawa and had similar hair, dark and shoulder length. She tucked her green skirt underneath her as she sat down. "Please sit," she said.

Sawa sat and explained about the two mysterious people in the hospital and presented the key to the manager. She looked at it. Sawa thought she looked at it a little too long as she must have seen these on a daily basis.

"I'm afraid I can't help you," Ming finally said, slowly looking up at Sawa.

"Why?" frowned Sawa. "It's our only clue as to who these people are."

"It may not be their key, and we have a policy on these particular keys that only written authority will allow a third party to access," insisted Ming.

"What about police?" said Sawa.

"Again, no, unless a judge issues an order if related to a serious crime." They stared at each other momentarily, and being both of Far East mentality, Sawa knew that it was pointless trying to negotiate. She stood up and was about to leave when Ming asked for the key, explaining it was the property of the bank.

Sawa smiled. "You had better ask Doctor Smith," she said, and left abruptly with the key.

Ming followed, but let her go. She then called the police and asked to talk with Detective Gunn.

"Gunn," answered the detective. The phone line wasn't clear, but he could understand, and faked surprise at the 'key' conversation from Ming. He told her he would let her know of any developments and that he would put it on the record.

"Thank you," said Ming, unconvinced, and put the phone down.

Two calls a few hours apart about a key, thought Gunn. "This sounds interesting," he said out loud and made his way out of the police station.

Gunn left for Nathon Hospital which was only a few minutes away past the tourist ferry port. Avoiding the military-style disembarkation comprising line after line of backpackers heading off the jetty from a recent ferry arrival to search out paradise beaches, Gunn arrived at the hospital car park. From here another beautiful beach could be seen but would remain undiscovered. The wind was fresh and the day hot and humid, which made Gunn sweat a little.

He made his way through the casualty department and to the reception next to the restaurant, which overlooked a central garden. The staff explained how to find Doctor Smith, alerting Gunn that he may be on his rounds. Taking two steps at a time, the skinny 37-year-old detective got to the first floor, found the doctor's door, and knocked. His receptionist poked her head around *her* door and told the detective that he would have to wait about five minutes, so best wait with her, which he did.

The air-conditioning worked well fighting the relentless external heat whilst Gunn looked out the window trying to remember the circumstances of their last encounter.

He recollected the strange murder case of bodies that were never found. Doctor Smith had informed Gunn that there were two types of blood, and the sheer volume of loss equated to death as no one could survive such haemorrhaging. So, two people were presumed dead and buried somewhere.

Nobody came forward with information and the owner of the house where the blood lay had all the right answers, which didn't sit well in Gunn's mind. He felt as if he were being played and there were some serious monied forces behind the scenes. The case remained unsolved and still bothered Gunn, whose thoughts were now interrupted by Doctor Smith's entrance.

"Detective Pyong, or Gunn?" said the doctor sarcastically.

"Please call me Gunn... I prefer that." (Pyong followed the Thai tradition of changing his birth name so evil gods could not find him.)

"No problem," said the doctor patting Gunn on the back in a friendly manner. "So serious! Hey, thank you for coming. Please come into my office. Coffee, tea, water?"

"Water will be fine," replied Gunn, and they made their way through the connecting door to Doctor Smith's office. Gunn thought the decoration to be of an old colonial style with wooden panelled walls adorned with plants, photos, and memorabilia.

"Long time," said Doctor Smith. "What is it, how many years? Goodness that's gone quick," he said answering his own question, "we were young then."

"We still are," interrupted Gunn with a smile.

"*You* maybe, looking so young, but sadly I have not fared so well."

Gunn liked the Englishman's honesty, which is why they got on so well.

"Anyway," Smith continued whilst running his fingers through his white hair, "I requested your presence regarding these two strange patients I talked about, if that is indeed what they are. Do you have any ideas?"

"No ideas at this time," replied Gunn.

Doctor Smith pointed out that that seemed to be a *de rigueur* answer in this particular case and perhaps Gunn could see the couple in question, upstairs, which was agreed.

They stared down at the couple in Room 22. The girl's hair was messy and long and the man was of similar state except he had a full dark beard.

"The reason I thought you may have some ideas about these two is this," and the doctor removed the bedsheet. Gunn instantly recognised stab wounds and asked when they had been inflicted.

"No idea," and the doctor laughed at his own response. "I mean, they were stitched up some time ago but it's not clear when, or where, for that matter."

"The stitching looks fresh," said Gunn referring to the recent punctures around the wounds.

"Oh no, stitches were removed, they looked awful and for some reason old. Hence the fresh blood marks."

"OK," said Gunn watching the motionless bodies who were both on drip feeds, "and the other one?"

"Same, except they are slash marks and one stab."

"Looks like one was seriously injured whilst one fought, I wonder in which order. Maybe the man tried to kill the girl?"

"Didn't think of that," said the doctor.

Gunn looked at the two bodies for a moment and deduced that the same knife was used on both victims, which would therefore equate to a third party. "Who brought them in?"

14

Smiling, Doctor Smith replied, "Once again, no idea. According to the nurse on duty they materialised in an instant... within minutes, out of nowhere." Gunn looked at the doctor and gave him a hard stare. Doctor Smith went on to explain the circumstances.

"So did Scotty beam them down?" said Gunn seriously.

Knowing what Gunn was referring to, Smith still asked what he meant.

"Star Trek, Kirk, The Starship Enterprise...?" Gunn responded raising his eyebrows at the doctor.

"I thought you meant that," replied Doctor Smith, "but you looked so serious. I misjudged your understanding of English, which is very good, by the way." (Gunn, unbeknown to the doctor, had studied police forensics in the UK where his fellow students enlightened him as to English self-deprecation and irony.)

"Do you have any better ideas?" Gunn asked, "and thank you." They both realised that a man of science and a seasoned detective had no other answers to combat the Star Trek theory. Gunn thought this could be a long case if this was the starting block.

He got up to leave and abruptly sat down again. "Oh, what about the key?"

"Ah yes, the key, I almost forgot, we believe it's for a safety deposit box in . Siam Bank. I sent Nurse Sawa earlier to try and find out what was in there, but she said we had no authority – so no luck. They said they wanted to retain the key."

"And did they?"

"Yes."

"So, Nurse Sawa went to which branch...?" queried Gunn.

"Chaweng, it had the phone number on the tag."

"Any name or reference on it?"

Doctor Smith thought Gunn had a lot of questions to what seemed like an afterthought. He answered, "No reference, no."

"And now you don't have the key?"

Doctor Smith now felt like he was under investigation and replied slightly irritated, "No, Gunn. I don't have the key."

"OK," smiled Gunn reassuringly and got up to leave.

"What are we to do now?" asked the doctor.

"We wait for them to wake up. In the meantime, I'll go visit the bank. I'll let you know."

On his way out, Nurse Sawa was preparing to come in. "Oh, Gunn, this is Nurse Sawa."

"Pleased to meet you," said Gunn, and left.

1998. Questions with no answers

The next day Gunn left his villa overlooking the sea near Nathon. The villa was impressive and built by his English father who had married his Thai mother soon after it was finished. Gunn was an only child and now he was technically an orphan. He didn't have many friends and up to now remained unmarried even though he was a bit of a ladies' man. He liked to joke around which confused the Thais, as self-deprecation is seen as a sign of stupidity and, worse still, weakness. Gunn preferred the English way and missed his English friends who didn't need his special brand of humour explained.

He headed down the shortest route to Chaweng along the well-made coast road. He arrived at Siam Bank at around 11am and asked to see Ming. She showed him to her office, and she relived the conversation (in their native language) that she had had with Sawa.

"Have you checked inside the box?"

"No. It's against our protocol," replied Ming.

"OK, but you do know who it belongs to?" pressed Gunn.

"Yes, it's a company called 'Chourne Gora'."

"Strange name," said Gunn pensively. He started to try and figure out the connection with the couple and he'd hoped the name might reveal one of the people in room 22.

"You OK?" asked Ming.

"Yes, fine. How long has this box been occupied by your client? Does it have a name or number?"

"22..."

"What?!" said Gunn, interrupting, sitting suddenly upright.

"Box 22, why the surprise?" asked Ming, noticing Gunn's response.

Gunn stared at Ming to see if her actions revealed anything else but surprise. But they did not. She didn't know the connection.

"And, how long?" Gunn continued.

"About 20 years."

"Wow, that's a long time. Do they open it regularly?"

"No, only once after it was opened, I believe. I checked the history after Sawa had been."

"I don't suppose you can give me the name of the individual?"

Ming shook her head. "You know the answer, no. Sorry."

"How soon after?"

"What?"

"...Was the box revisited."

"Oh, about a week."

"Then nothing?"

"Actually, no there's a record of a second visit more recently," mused Ming, "but I have to check when."

Gunn paused. "So how many keys to the box?"

"Three."

"Three. And you have two?"

"No. One!"

Gunn didn't reveal his confusion at the answer and continued what was clearly an interrogation.

"But there are three, where are the other two?"

"The client has one and Nurse Sawa... or Dr Smith, who I believe sent her."

"Really," said Gunn calmly. After a pause he said, "OK that's all I need for now." He stood up and asked to be informed if anybody should visit or enquire about the box. Ming nodded her head and opened the door for Gunn. As she turned to go back to her desk, Gunn came back in.

"Sorry, do you have the details of the Chourne Gora company?"

"I do but only as much as you can find on the internet... they have a web page."

"Oh, right, thank you. Have a good day."

1998. Mojito Island

Gunn decided to have lunch at The Red Snapper, a highly reputable restaurant on the beach side of the street, to mull over this very confusing situation. He was known here, and the service reflected his popularity. He had something on the three main mafia bosses, who respected Gunn, and that fact was known amongst all the establishments along the nearby Cheong Mon, Chaweng and Bohput beach fronts.

He paid his bill and decided to go and see O, the owner of O.P. Bungalows. These had a prime spot on the beach, one of the first bungalow hotels to open on Chaweng. O was in herself a bit of an institution and Gunn liked her calm controlled way of dealing with situations. Here Gunn occasionally shared a beer with her on the separate seafront bar where he now took a seat. O saw Gunn and came over with a beer for him.

"Sawasdee ka," she said putting her hands in an inverted Y shape and bowing her head, in the traditional Thai greeting known as a wai. "Hi O," said Gunn. He nodded towards a floating shaded structure tended by a barman. "What's that?"

"Our new bar on the sea, it's called Mojito Island."

"It looks amazing," said Gunn. The bar had a white canvas canopy and freshly cut palm leaves around it's sides. Beside it were floating white leatherette beds with lounging customers sipping drinks, served by a waitress wading knee deep through the water. '

"It's owned by a man called Peter Snelson. He pays me rent. He lives here. Not a bad idea, huh!"

"Not bad at all. Never seen anything like it. I must jump on sometime."

"You must. What brings you here today?" O asked.

"I had a meeting at Siam Bank, do you know the manageress, Khun Ming? It was with her."

"Yes, she comes sometimes. You a customer or has there been a robbery?"

Gunn smiled. "Not sure. Maybe – maybe not, but I'm not a customer." He leant over a little towards O. "There are two people who have appeared out of nowhere in a Nathon Hospital room who have a connection to this branch."

"Oh, that sounds strange," O replied.

Gunn went on to explain his predicament. O sat back and said, "No idea."

"Funny, that's what everyone says," said Gunn smiling and sipping his beer. "Thing is, who's the liar? Let me know if you see anything odd. I have a little feeling a hornet's nest has been disturbed," and he stood up and wai'd O. "Watch Ming," he said as he left to walk down the sandy drive.

1998. More lies?

Gunn waited a while after returning to the hospital and Nurse Sawa turned up at the hospital canteen. He watched her get a tray and buy her lunch. She paid then turned around to look for a free table and caught Gunn's eyes. Her surprised smile gave away a lot to a seasoned detective like Gunn; to him it read '*Oh no, here we go*'. She skirted around a few seated nurses and sat in front of Gunn overlooking the glass enclosed courtyard gardens.

"Sawasdee Ka," she said and gave Gunn an emotionless smile.

"Sawasdee Krup," replied Gunn. Good food here?"

"It's OK; what can I do for you? I guess you're here to see me or do you eat here regularly?" said Sawa, now unsmiling.

"No… I don't – I came to see a friend," lied Gunn, deciding to change his original attack plan to pacification.

"Ah! How's the investigation?"

"Confusing."

"How so?" said Sawa trying to catch Gunn's eye.

"Missing keys or keys that have their own life," said Gunn looking down at his sandwich. "You know about keys, don't you?"

"I presume you're talking about the bank safety deposit box?" Sawa picked up Gunn's sarcastic tone and readied herself.

"I am. I've been informed you still have one," said Gunn, looking hard at Sawa.

Sawa, unmoved by the stare, replied, "I did, but I gave it back to the bank."

This answer was half-expected by Gunn. He had hoped this would not be the reply as a whole host of new avenues now opened up. It did however eliminate Doctor Smith.

"Oh, I thought you may have forgotten to give it back to Doctor Smith," continued Gunn.

"No, I gave it to the receptionist. The manager asked for it back and I said no but thought otherwise, so put it on the table by the receptionist before I left."

Wow, this girl covers her bases, she is definitely up to something, thought Gunn in an instant.

"Really."

"Yes, really," said Sawa.

"I best be on my way... lots of doors to knock on. That's what detectives do you know. Hey, have a good lunch, and nice meeting you. By the way how are the Room 22 occupants?"

"I will. The occupants haven't moved. Good luck in your search," wished Sawa without any warmth.

"Thank you." And Gunn left to make a call to the bank.

The key was missing or lost and/or people were lying. *Why?* Gunn wondered. *There must be inside information about what was in that box. Unless the key had been lost and this was all an innocent chain of events. There was no crime as such.*

He didn't believe the latter.

1998. Decisions

Sawa had the key in a safe place and was wondering about its importance. She was not rich and coming from a poor farming village near Chiang Mai, life had taught her to identify things of worth. She felt the key to be such a thing as the circumstances by which it appeared were extraordinary.

She had been promised a small fortune to conceal it, which she now had done, and had been told to await further instructions. This came in the form of a note plus 50,000 Thai Baht (which was about £1000) as a sweetener having appeared under her door. She knew Gunn would be on to her after he checked out Ming, concluding that Ming really didn't have a clue about the key's whereabouts. This would lead him to her. And soon.

***

Sawa didn't quite realise how soon. Unbeknown to her, Gunn was on his way. In the darkness, as the sun had recently set behind the mountains of Chaweng, Gunn was now cruising past Beach Temple. Sawa lived off the Ghost Road near the junction which led to the big, isolated Macro supermarket. Gunn was fast approaching this when he received a call on his mobile. It was Doctor Smith.

Gunn pulled over and asked Doctor Smith what he was talking about, whereupon he made a decision to go immediately back to Nathon hospital. It took him 40 minutes and he hated this particular drive as it was so boring to him – the opposite view of the many tourists who did the same journey marvelling at the mauve silhouette of the *Full Moon Party* island of Koh Phangan across the turquoise sea. He finally got to the deserted hospital and ran up the stairs to Doctor Smith's office.

"Detective Gunn, we now have a *really big* mystery," said Doctor Smith to the out of breath man.

"When did it happen or when did you realise?" asked Gunn.

"About an hour ago."

"Can I see?"

"Sure, come with me. I still can't believe it," Doctor Smith continued as they hurried along the corridors.

"Who told you?"

"One of the duty nurses phoned my secretary. I went immediately and told the ward staff to do a thorough search."

"And...?"

"Nothing."

They arrived at Room 22. It was empty.

1998. Strange journey

Nurse Sawa was escorted from her small one-bedroomed stilted bungalow after answering a knock on the door. Her departure was not voluntary, and she was helped into the back of a black SUV by two men, one of whom drove.

"What's this about?" asked Sawa as they passed Big C supermarket. They were heading in the direction of Lamai beach which was about 20 minutes away when they suddenly turned off the road and headed back on themselves, except the route was along narrow dusty roads.

"You lost them?" asked the man in the back with Sawa.

"Yes," said the driver wearing a white T-shirt and straw hat.

Sawa was concerned but not scared as this was obviously about the key. She had an ace card. She had copied the key, which no one knew about. The hidden one would fit, and she was holding the copy. The real one was at the hospital tucked into her office chair. She figured if the police became a problem, she could always *find* it and claim it was all a misunderstanding. She had given instructions to her friend Doctor Jah to disclose this information should things get serious.

The men didn't answer Sawa's original question, and they continued to drive in silence which she could see was towards Big Buddha. They came off a main road and pulled over.

"Time to put this on," said the backseat man and passed her a blindfold which she calmly placed over her head, covering her eyes. The man then placed a cowboy hat inclined at a forward angle so that she couldn't see if the blindfold failed and tied her hands in front of her. They then drove up and down many little roads so Sawa would be disorientated. The car stopped. She heard some gates open, and the car proceeded momentarily, only to stop again. After a short wait she again heard wooden gates close behind her as she was eased out. They walked over what felt to her like a humped wooden bridge. Another set of footsteps joined the group, although they didn't sound right to Sawa. Another door opened and she was led into a room and sat down. The unusual footsteps faded away to nothing along the way.

She could hear the men leaving and then there was silence. She was now afraid but in a strange way, as she felt an unnatural, almost ghostly presence – which made her shiver.

She sat motionless in her darkness wondering what fate had lined up for her for about three minutes – then a man in front of her spoke.

"Hello Sawa," he said in a quiet voice, which she recognised was an English accent. Not your regular English accent, she surmised. She realised he must have been sitting there watching her all this time, which gave her the creeps.

"Am I safe?" she asked.

"Perfectly safe," he paused, "provided you keep your side of the bargain."

She sat facing the voice when slowly the right-hand side of her face became very cold. Ice cold. Something breathed out and paused.

"GET... out... of... here," a female voice whispered slowly in her ear. This made Sawa's skin crawl, but she dared not move. The man tilted his head, and he noticed a condensation mist appear by Sawa's ear for no apparent reason in the hot stuffy room.

Sawa breathed out suddenly and asked out loud, "How many people are here?"

Confused by the question the man said, "Only me." He put his glass down on the table and sat back.

Sawa turned her head, still unable to see. "Only you?"

"What are you talking about? Why would you care how many? I'm here to question you, in case you didn't understand," said the man, slightly agitated.

The man noticed that Sawa had turned white and was shivering. This confused him and stared at her intensely trying to understand the condensation. "Are you OK?"

His concern seemed odd but reassuring and her face started to warm up. "Yes, I'm fine."

"The key. Where did you put it?"

"How do I know who you are?" she asked, which was a reasonable question, thought the man.

"Notes under your door and 50,000 Baht should ring a bell. So, where's the key?" he pressed, raising his voice.

Taking heed of the unidentified girl's whisper, Sawa decided to play things straight and get out of there. She replied, "If you take me away from here towards Chaweng and remove my blindfold, I'll tell you."

The man thought for a second, "OK," he said.

1998. An escape?

Sawa was led out of the room by the same man who had brought her in, known as Atai. She recognised his aftershave, although she felt there was another soft set of footsteps, following behind. Her skin again shivered at the temperature drop. These footsteps didn't belong to one of *them*. Her interrogator had remained in the room.

"Hello," she said, turning her head blindly.

"I'm here, not there," said her escort laughing. "No cavalry back there!"

What was going on in this place? thought Sawa. The car engine started, and she was helped back in. The interrogation room door closed, and she heard the interrogator follow. A second car was brought up and he said to Atai, "Follow her instructions," before he got in. The cars left and Sawa breathed out. She had felt incredibly bad energy back there.

They drove a while and then her blindfold was removed whereupon she realised they were now approaching Chaweng Beach – recognising the Karma Hotel on the way. The cars pulled over on the quiet, wide, dark road. "OK, where is it?"

"How can I guarantee my money if I tell you?" asked Sawa nervously.

"You will have to trust us."

Sawa thought for a moment, realising her limited options, and told of the key's location at OP Bungalows and the big tree on the beach. The driver got out of the car and went to the parked car behind to explain and receive his orders. Sawa was now very afraid about what the driver's instructions were as she had no more cards to play in their eyes. The driver closed the door and said, "Big Man said we wait here," and turned off the engine. Relieved Sawa collapsed back into her seat. She was going to live, for now.

***

Detective Gunn was driving back along the coast road completely confused by the circumstances of the now empty Room 22. *Where on earth have they gone? Someone must have seen them. They were naked so where did they get the clothes from? Getting dressed unnoticed in such a busy ward would be extraordinary. There must be another party...* All these unanswered questions in Gunn's mind shortened the journey back to Chaweng that bored him so much.

He turned into the Ghost Road and passed the point he was at a few hours earlier. He pulled up to Nurse Sawa's house and sat in the car outside with the engine off, a few metres away on the other side of the road. He breathed out and surveyed the other shabby houses in the dimly lit dusty road, all of which were no more than small wooden shacks. It was now 11.30pm and the new moon provided little light.

He wasn't sure what he was up against, and experience had taught him to be careful when treading into the unknown. Confident he wasn't being watched, he got out of the car and slowly made his way to Sawa's house, where he climbed the few dusty stairs that led to her modest wooden balcony. He looked back and then went to knock on Sawa's door, which he noticed wasn't completely closed. This now didn't feel right at all to Gunn, but he decided to push the door a little anyway. It opened and he could make out a bed in the small dark room.

"Nurse Sawa?" Gunn said softly. There was silence.

***

Nurse Sawa had now been waiting for at least half an hour with her unsavoury companions in the car, who said nothing. Occasional cars raced past them with their headlights dazzling them, otherwise it was quiet, dark and still. They were away from the clubs and bars of Chaweng, so there were no passers-by either.

"Who's the Big Man?" asked Sawa, trying her luck.

The man in the front turned around and looked menacingly at her and then smiled. "None of your business," he said in a calm voice.

"Will you let me go after you get the key?" Sawa asked, realising that the answer was no longer obvious. The man turned away. Sawa was once again becoming a little frightened as she began to feel that this was a big deal – realising her life to be in danger if they discovered that the key was a fake. She originally thought that the key was her chance to make money but dying had not been part of the equation. So now it was decision time. Tell them about the fake or see how the dice would fall when they found out. She remembered a patient once saying to her after being shot, *"Dead men don't wear seatbelts."* She never fully understood the meaning but felt it had some relevance now.

Sawa chose a third way.

"I need to go to the toilet."

The man looked into the rear-view mirror and said nothing.

"I need to go to the toilet," Sawa repeated calmly. "Now!"

The driver considered the options and looked at his companion. He nodded.

"Ok lady, come with me."

The driver remained seated and the other opened the door for Sawa. She got out.

"I can go over there?" she said, pointing with her tied hands to a passage.

He nodded and untied her hands before he started to walk with her.

"You wanna watch?" said Sawa sarcastically and the man responded by stopping.

She continued briefly to the passage which ran down the side of the hotel. Sawa knew this led to the sea. She didn't look back until she felt he was out of sight. Then she walked quickly away from the scene towards the sea which crashed onto the beach. She started to run – this was now a deception and an action which could not be passed off as a misunderstanding. A decision made which if wrong could lead to death. The chase was on!

The man shouted to hurry up and received no answer which made him suspicious. The driver got out of the car. "What's going on?" and he walked quickly past the man towards the passage. The man sheepishly followed. She was gone!

"You fucking idiot!" shouted Atai and they both ran down the passage towards the crashing sea. She was nowhere to be seen. They looked left and right and instinctively split up and ran in opposite directions.

Sawa had turned right and ran into the walled gardens of the hotel following a path behind which led towards the headland rocks. There was a couple in the distance who she tried to hide from by staying low as she ran. She hid behind a bush under a palm tree anticipating the men to be entering the gardens imminently. One man came into view and bent over, out of breath.

Sawa stiffened. Upon noticing the couple, the man made his way to them, and they spoke briefly. Sawa couldn't hear anything but the breaking waves behind, but saw the couple shake their heads. The man then turned around suddenly and looked in Sawa's direction. Sawa quickly realised he had no idea what he was looking at and remained stationary. The man then slowly directed his gaze across the rest of the gardens and remained still whilst he did so. *Animals that move in nature are quickly spotted by their hunters,* so Sawa didn't move.

She knew she had a potential dangerous second front! The other man might still be on the beach running in her direction. The noisy sea compromised her sense of hearing which was a serious sense to lose in the situation, so she remained in the bushes. This brief respite seemed to last an eternity, which gave her an inkling that the men must have split up. Sawa's heart was pounding as she wasn't oblivious to the fact that these moments could be her last.

The man finally moved and started to come towards her which made her heart race even more. She remembered another expression about an animal being caught by a predator: *At what point does food realise that it is food?* She got ready to run but inexplicably the man turned around and started to retrace his steps. She crouched lower and watched, deciding in that moment to dash for the rocks on the headland, which she knew well from her childhood. From there she could use her knowledge of the terrain to her advantage. The new moon would provide cover instead of casting shadows on the sand.

Then to her horror she saw the other man enter the gardens.

The Second Handshake

1990. Christmas. London

Julian was sitting in a pub positioned on a snowy, cobbled back alley behind the Kings Road, well known to black cab drivers as a sneaky cut through. It was an institution of a pub, generally frequented by local eccentrics (who talked about the past and better times), the artistic, and the upwardly mobile.

The low ceilings created a cosy claustrophobia with daub and wattle plastered walls set between heavy wooden support beams. These had been hastily adorned for Christmas with tinsel and expensive candles. A lovingly decorated Christmas tree sat by the small bar in the corner next to the well-attended fire. It was a tourist's dream image of an English institution. Julian, in a world of his own, gazed out through the lattice Georgian windows at the ever-increasing snowy flurry outside.

"It'll never happen."

"What?" said Julian slightly taken aback and looked sideways across the apex of the bar where a young man of about twenty stood. He was paying for his drink.

"You look like the world is on your shoulders," continued the young man.

"That obvious, eh!...no just life, you know?" replied Julian.

"Sometimes. My name is Gunn."

"Julian," and he leant over to shake Gunn's hand. "That's a fine tan you got there, where's that from, not Croydon that's for sure."

"No," laughed Gunn, "you got a thing for Croydon?"

"Well, it's not that sunny there and I always said that when Hitler was bombing they should have turned all the lights on in Croydon to help the bombers focus."

Gunn laughed again.

"Where are you from?" asked Julian.

"Thailand. My father is English."

"Oh wow, wish I was there now," replied Julian. "What you doing in England? Holiday?"

"No, I'm studying police forensics." Said Gunn receiving change from the barmaid for his drinks.

"Detective Gunn...you should be in a book. Gunn gets loaded in a bar," said Julian and laughed.

"Perhaps I should...don't follow the loaded bit though?" said Gunn, a little confused.

"It's an expression in England, for getting drunk, loaded..." confirmed Julian.

"Oh, I see, yes that's funny. Look, I'm really sorry, I'd love to talk but I have to go, I was on my way out. People waiting. Nice talking to you though."

"You too, said Julian. I'll look you up when I come to Thailand one day."

"You do that. Koh Samui, Nathon Police Station... probably. I'll be waiting," and Gunn left.

"Koh Samui," repeated Julian to himself silently, shaking his head with a grin imagining the palm trees and beaches.

In the background Julian heard a customer pulling the barman's leg, "Hey Terry, what do you call a boomerang that doesn't work?"

The Australian barman replied, "Go on," expecting the worst. "A stick," which was followed by drunken laughter.

The barman retorted, "What do you call a guy who's had too much to drink?"

"Go on, tell me," slurred the customer.

"A cab," and the barman raised his eyebrows and walked away as the customers laughed.

A cold wind blew the snow into the bar, briefly releasing a sudden chill that cut through the fickle heat from the fire, disturbing the cotton wool hum of the few people talking in the other bar. Someone had come in from outside.

"Merry Christmas!"

Disturbed once again from his thoughts, Julian looked around. It was his brother Damian who had come through the other door.

"Oh, hi, cheers! Thanks for coming."

***

Earlier when Julian was putting his laundry in his drawers, he had found one of his old black and white school photographs. It was in his underwear drawer which had slowly been infested by migrating socks. The neatly folded shirts in the drawer below had become a mess after many hurried forays to find something to wear for an impromptu night out. So, chaos reigned.

When Julian picked up the photograph the room became very warm – almost tropical – causing him to let go of the photo and stand upright, to look around, wondering where on earth the unusual heat was coming from. Time stood still as he momentarily imagined looking across a tropical sea at a deserted small island. Then the heat stopped and slightly confused he looked down to pick up the photo, but it wasn't there. He looked through all the drawers, creating even more havoc in the shirt drawer, but to no avail. Despite the facts, he chose to presume that there had to be a rational explanation and decided to get on with his day. Perhaps he had imagined it, but the photo remained a mystery.

***

Saviour's Day by Cliff Richard had reached number one and was playing across the room in the pub.

"They'll be playing this in 2000 years' time," said Julian.

"What do you mean?" asked Damien, smirking, "It's only about three minutes long."

"Ha, ha. Good one. They play the same songs from Christmas past over and over, smart ass," continued Julian. "They become an institution."

"Oh!" said Damien sarcastically.

"I mean," continued Julian ignoring Damien, "imagine not playing Slade at Christmas? Ever!"

"True." Damien tried to catch the eye of the barmaid, who was struggling to tame a gherkin which had escaped its jar on the counter.

"I mean, Slade, 20 years old and counting. Only 1880 years to go if I'm only half correct. More!"

Damien smiled at his younger brother. "If that's all you got to worry about you must be having a good day."

"Weird day, actually," and Julian explained the photograph and heat story.

Damien finally ordered a coffee and Julian waited for him to do so before he spoke.

"Thanks for coming."

"No problem, what's up? You look like you could do with a holiday."

"Tell me about it," said Julian, wearily, and their heads turned as the door opened again.

A young couple came in from the worsening blizzard where 1990 looked like it was going to break the mould, and a cosy white winter was on the cards. The couple dusted themselves off, stamping their feet, and put their coats on the partially full coat rack. The girl made her way to the fire giving Julian a lingering look as she passed which didn't go unnoticed by Damien. Her boyfriend went to the polished mahogany bar.

"Know her, do ya?" teased Damien.

"What d'ya mean?" Julian replied, coyly pretending not to have noticed.

"Well, she seems to know you... you're not that good looking!" said Damien, grinning.

"Funny, she actually does look familiar... her eyes..." He glanced back over his shoulder and saw her back as she warmed herself in front of the fire.

She turned and walked towards a chosen small round table, only this time staring straight ahead until her boyfriend joined her with two hot chocolates, laced with rum. He handed one to the girl.

"Cheers, G," said Nastya.

1990. The brothers

Julian gave a lingering stare at the attractive couple and then turned to Damien and said, "I feel as if I'm in a spot of bother, but I can't put my finger on it."

"What do you mean? Are you in trouble?" asked Damien.

"I don't know. I feel as if I've stumbled onto something I shouldn't have."

"Really? What? Sounds exciting."

"I picked it up from my newspaper job," Julian explained.

"How's that going? Fleet Street beckons. The new wonder journalist!"

"Probably not quite now, I doubt *The Richmond Times* is due to take over *The Telegraph* just yet. Anyway. Odd stuff has been happening as well. Strange things, stuff... for example, you see the couple sitting down over there?"

Damien looked around slowly, "Yeah, she's nice."

"I know them. Or at least I feel as if I do, except I've never met them before. I get these ongoing *déjà vu* feelings. A lot. Sometimes many in a row."

Damien stared at Julian over his coffee for a second, not knowing what to say. It certainly wasn't an answer he expected from his level-headed brother.

"Really?" was the best he could come up with.

"I was doing this article thing on Health and Safety – a moan, basically – and checked when it was enshrined into law. I found it was gradual and picked up that the name Reklem kept appearing. Naturally I wondered why he or she should be involved in UK Health and Safety issues, so I've been checking around trying to find the connection. I feel as if I shouldn't have. It also turned out Reklem was a *she*."

They became distracted by the barmaid continuing to do her chores, only this time wrestling with some chips that kept falling off a plate. 'New' thought Damien. They heard the doors close, and Julian's eyes shifted to an empty table. The young couple had left.

"Beer? Brandy?"

"Better idea," said Damien.

"So, after more digging it turns out this Reklem seems to be linked to a Conservative called Gerry Absalom," said Julian. "Turns out Gerry isn't a Tory at all really, quite the reverse. He's a Trot. He's also taken quite an interest in our gold reserves. Don't ask me why but there's a connection I feel. I gather he wants to sell the gold - from snippets of information which I come across. Don't ask me how or why. I feel as if I'm being fed a path of information from someone. But here's the thing – he's also interested in selling Europe's gold as well. Gerry Absalom's been doing the rounds of other European leaders and instigating gold sales of their countries. I'm not sure where to look next. It doesn't look right. And, well, I think I'm being monitored."

"What?"

"My mail seems as if it's been opened prior to me receiving it," said Julian.

"Really? Do you have a source?"

"I'm definitely being *fed* information, which is the puzzling thing – it's very obvious, as if someone wants me to find a trail but feel as if it's my discovery."

"Why not wait a while, see what happens..." said Damien reassuringly.

1993. Lisa's snow

It was another winter in London when Lisa turned on her heels and said goodbye to her young friend Nastya. The grey skies were darkening, and the beginnings of a snowy blizzard were very apparent. The temperature dropped and the wind picked up, indicating a new weather front was upon the city. Slowly and then suddenly, the wispy flakes emboldened and started to get a grip, turning the newly laid slush white. Lisa loved the snow and took her time walking as it was so peaceful and quiet. She found and leant on a fence overlooking a tiny, snow-coated green, and decided she preferred snow over sun anytime.

Suddenly she jumped and shouted, turning around with her fists in the air, startled by a pinch on her bottom. She again looked behind her, and around, but no one or anything was there. She looked down at the fresh snowy ground and only saw her footprint trail leading to where she stood. There were no others! Whatever or whoever pinched her – and it *was* a pinch, of that there was no doubt – must have been floating from above, which was clearly nonsense. Frowning and standing upright in the dimly lit snow, she continued looking all around her but to no avail. There wasn't a soul! A shiver ran down her back, which had nothing to do with the weather.

Slowly, she walked back retracing her footprints. Shrugging her shoulders, she changed direction and instead walked towards a turning, leading to a pedestrian alley and entered a bookshop/café. The Georgian bow frontage with lattice windows gave the whole place a Dickensian feel. She ordered a black coffee and sat perplexed on a chair by a table overlooking the snowy Notting Hill scenery from the safety of the warm, stuffy establishment.

Such an occurrence wasn't a total surprise to Lisa due to her understanding of the Shoestring theory in Quantum Gravity. In the world of black holes even time travel existed. However, it was still disconcerting when confronted face to face with such strange phenomena.

She had learnt that 'A moving clock ticks more slowly the closer it approaches the speed of light', which features in the time dilation of Special Relativity. Time and infinity are inseparable and infinity fascinated Lisa. She was obsessed with when things began and ended *– the second something stops can be split into two half-seconds... again and again to infinity, meaning the absolute point at which something stops is impossible to determine.*

This intense study made Lisa realise that time travel, ghosts, past lives, *déjà vu,* and the like was *the* reality, not just a possibility. This understanding empowered her mind.

The snow had really taken hold now, and the traffic at the end of the alley was moving slowly creating a ghostly haze of red taillights and fuzzy headlights. It was at this moment whilst Lisa was thumbing through one of the books in the café's 'library' that a postcard became dislodged and fell onto the table in front of her. She put the book down and picked the card up.

The postcard was very old and displayed a faded photo collage of a beach.

"Ahem," said a stranger standing over her, "do you mind if I sit here?"

"Err, no, of course go ahead, sorry I was distracted."

"So, I see," said the man, taking a seat. Nodding towards the card, he added, "Thailand?"

"What?" said Lisa.

"I reckon that's Chaweng beach, you been there? It's in Thailand"

"No," said Lisa, unsure although for some reason she felt she had a connection with the place.

"You should go sometime, it's nice. It's in Koh Samui, although I have to say that it looks very odd – it's very built up. Don't recognise half of it. It's as if it's in the future. How old's the card?" He was now straining his neck to stare at it.

"Don't know... Perhaps I'll go sometime, thank you." And the conversation stopped. The man focused on his drink and looked out the window.

Lisa flipped the yellowed card over. There was an address on it which was partially obscured by the country stamp. There was something else, but she couldn't quite put her finger on it. She stared at it for a while, sipping her coffee, avoiding the occasional glances from the stranger who was clearly keen to strike up a conversation. There was a sketch of five palm trees and a house with an arrow pointed at it.

She tried to figure out what it might have been about. A treasure map crossed her mind, and she gave a wry smile. *'Probably no'*, thought to herself. She got up from her chair whilst giving the stranger a glancing smile and left. The snow was forming drifts, and the flakes were like chunky cotton wool which obscured her vision when they landed near her eyes. It was cold. She checked behind her for any bottom pinchers but there were none.

***.

Later in a café Lisa said to Nastya, "It's as if the card was meant for me," holding the card in front of her.

1993. The Travel Agent

Nastya woke up suddenly in the night. A thought crossed her mind, and she went to the living room. It was too early to call anybody so she went back to bed and lay down, wide awake and wishing the next four hours away so she could ring Lisa at eight.

She eventually dialled out and got hold of a very dozy Lisa. "You're early," she said.

"Sorry," said Nastya.

"Are we meeting today then?"

"Yes, but something's come up."

"What?" said Lisa, expecting a cancellation.

"You know the postcard you found?"

"Yes,"

"Not sure how to say this, but I thought about the writing..."

"Okaaay..."

***

They met shortly after the mysterious conversation in a Hammersmith café near Ravenscourt Park.

"You got the card?"

"Yes..." said Lisa, reservedly.

"Give it to me."

Nastya almost grabbed the card from Lisa as she brought it out of her bag. She strained her eyes, looking very closely at the back of the card.

"Thought so."

"Thought so what?" said Lisa confused.

"It's my handwriting."

"Get outta here!"

"No... it really is. It really is," insisted Nastya, hardly believing it herself.

"What are you talking about? You are saying I found a card by chance in a book, in a weird café - then you say you wrote it??? You've never been to Thailand, let alone *Five Trees House*."

"I know."

"Then..."

"I don't know, I really don't. This is crazy I know, but I'm not making it up," said Nastya, "but all the little quirks in my writing match. It's mine."

They sat in silence for a second or two, when Lisa interjected "Here's some paper. Here's a pen. Write Five Trees House." Nastya obeyed and they both leaned forward to study the writing. It seemed like nonsense to both - but it matched.

"Do you know something? A strange sequence of events happened before I found the card. It's as if I was led there. I changed my mind on going home."

Lisa then proceeded to explain the mysterious bottom pinch.

"God if we told someone about this, they'd put us away... or at least leave pretty quickly," said Nastya.

"The guy in the shop said the photo was odd, as if it's been built up recently, implying that this had been written after the build...which hasn't happened yet."

"That makes as much sense as I don't know what! I wonder what that beach really looks like?" pondered Lisa.

"Here's an idea, why not go to a travel agent on King Street down the road? They'll have brochures," said Nastya.

"Great idea," enthused Lisa. They got their things together and went out into the cold where the snow wouldn't have looked out of place in Norway.

They went into the brightly lit travel agent promoting a different world of sun and beaches with happy, smiling people. They looked along the shelves full of glossy magazines, beckoning them to a great adventure. They asked the agent watching them if they had any Thailand brochures.

"Not many people go there, it's a long way – what makes you want to go there?" enquired the agent.

"Chaweng Beach, we were encouraged to visit. It's a place on a Koh Samui."

"Must be open season there," said the agent.

"Sorry?" questioned Nastya.

"You're the second lot of people to ask about it this week!"

"Right." said Lisa, uninterested.

"Anyway, I can show you your beach as I know exactly where to look," said the agent.

He flicked through a chosen magazine and stopped halfway. He then retraced a few pages and said, "Aha! Here we are, Chaweng."

The girls got the postcard and held it up to the brochure.

They all looked at it for a moment in silence.

"That can't be right," said the agent, "it's all built up!!"

"You sure it's Chaweng?" asked Lisa.

"Yes, it's got the same reef in front of the lagoon. See?"

"You're right. Then how come this is so built up?" said Nastya. You've got an old photo, of the future. That makes sense... not!"

Neither party could work this out.

"Maybe we can borrow the brochure?" asked Lisa finally.

"By all means, have it," said the confused agent.

"Thank you," said the girls simultaneously and left. The agent stood briefly trying to absorb what had just happened, and then returned to his desk shaking his head.

"What's this all about?" said Nastya.

"Beats me," said Lisa, "it's as if we've got a postcard from the future."

"Yeah. Written by me," said Nastya softly.

The girls went to Nastya's flat around the corner at Overstone Road. It was a basement flat in a semi-detached Victorian, three-story, flat-fronted house. They pushed open the heavy, wrought iron gate and made their way down the slightly perilous, steep flight of stairs.

They went into the living room in the small flat, which was gloomy at the best of times as the garden was higher than the windows. A large tree dominated the garden which had originally been planted as a seed to respect the memory of their dog. The family hadn't considered the location of the planting which had resulted in a misplaced huge tree. It should have been planted by the wall.

They sat down at the oak table which belonged to Nastya's parents.

"Nice tree," chuckled Lisa sarcastically.

"Long story," said Nastya, and returned to the matter in hand.

They quickly got the magazine out and started comparing the photos to the card. "It's the same place," said Lisa, breaking the silence.

"It is. It is, isn't it?"

"It is," reassured Lisa.

"The buildings are so amazing, so modern. Look at that pool. Weeeow! There's some people on what looks like mini walkie talkies... It's got the hotel name *Amari* over it. I guess that's the name we should find."

"Can we check if there's an Amari on Samui?" asked Nastya.

"Dunno," said Lisa, focused. "An international phone directory?"

"Brilliant, Lisa, brilliant!" enthused Nastya. "Where the fuck does one find that?"

They figured the travel agent would have one, or at least know where to find one.

They returned to the shop and the same agent stood up and smiled. "What can I do for you ladies? I don't understand what happened a while ago I must admit, was that some sort of trick?"

"We aren't totally sure ourselves, but that's for another day. Do you have an international phone directory by any chance?"

"We do, we always make international calls to hotels and tour operators', part of the job."

"Amazing," said Nastya, "would it be possible to call a number from here? We can pay you."

"I suppose you could, why not?! Let me guess — Thailand, Koh Samui?"

Nastya pointed her fingers in the form of a shooting gun at the agent, "Bang! You got it mista, do you mind?"

***

1993. The Swan

Julian received a letter out of the blue. It read: *'You were on the right lines, it's time now...'*

Julian turned left at something he considered to be hideously ugly – the Kingston *Peter Jones* department store – and walked along the unspoilt park on a mud footpath. The Thames here was serene, almost as if she were deep in thought, meandering effortlessly on a route worn into the landscape centuries ago. The odd swan glided past, disturbing the last of the mist which had settled overnight. The sun was bright but not strong, sending out a signal that better weather was on the way. That was exactly the mood Julian was in – upbeat, optimistic and happy.

He veered off from this part of old England after about fifteen minutes and walked to a house he was currently modernising. The happiness ebbed away as he pondered what horrors awaited him upon entering the front door. The sound of a jigsaw carved its way through the morning tranquillity of suburbia, alerting him that his builders must be on time for once. This sent a wave of relief through his veins, as it made for one less tedious discussion to have.

His phone rang just before he arrived at the front garden. It was his long-term friend Nick, a freelance journalist.

"Hey, how you doing?" said Julian, looking skyward at a half-finished roof.

"Great, just returning your call... everything ok?"

"Er, yeah!" said Julian, concerned at the scaffold construction above the roof.

Looking away, he continued "You won't believe what arrived on my doorstep this morning."

"What?"

"A note."

"What kind of note? A five-pound note or ..."

"No, it was a serious note, a confusing note, a note I don't fully understand..."

"Well go on, what did it say?"

"It said 'I was on the right track', and not to stop, er, 'now is the time.'"

Nick was silent for a moment and then said, "Is it about that stuff years ago?"

"I can't think of anything else; I *feel* it's about that."

"No name, signature... postcode?"

"No, nothing. Plus, it was hand-delivered!"

"Hmmm, interesting. What you up to for lunch by the way?"

"Nothing. Why, you around?"

"Yes, fancy *The Swan*?"

"Twickenham? On the river?"

"That's the one, say one-ish?"

"Deal. Let's talk then."

Julian refocused on the roof and stormed up the stairs to berate the builders.

The Swan had been frozen in time, thought Julian as he sat with his pint on the bench by a rising tidal Thames. He imagined Dick Turpin knocking back a few here before his next heist. He put his pint down on the picnic table and watched the riverbank's grass become gradually consumed by the clear, rising water. The pub overlooked the river, with a terrace and a further patio in front. Here Julian sat waiting.

Nick was late, but in such surroundings, Julian wasn't in any hurry - time seemed irrelevant to him at this moment. A smile appeared on his face when he noticed one of two girls sitting to the side of him casually glance his way for a moment too long – only to realise it herself and quickly turn her attention back to her chatty friend. Her friend, seeing her distraction, also shot a glance Julian's way and directly caught his eye. Then, embarrassed, she too carried on as if nothing happened.

"Got some admirers?" said Nick, interrupting the proceedings from behind him.

"You saw that did you?" said Julian, not realising that Nick had arrived. "I thought my flies were undone. Grab a seat. What can I get you?"

"A pint and the menu."

"Good idea!"

* * *

They sat and ate the delicious steak and kidney pie recommended by the barman.

"So, what you going to do?" said Nick.

"I've decided to carry on with my old investigation," said Julian. "Maybe I missed something before. Want to help?"

"Sure, doing what?"

"We'll see!"

"I did a quick check on the gold price earlier and it's doubled!"

"So has tax," quipped Nick.

"...And inflation," added Julian.

The two girls finished their drinks and got their things together whilst sliding their legs out from under the table. They had stopped talking to do so, and the first girl looked at Julian as they walked past. "Your purse!" Julian shouted out looking directly at her. "Your purse... it's on the table."

"Oh!" said the girl and went back to get it, with her unimpressed friend looking on at the oldest trick in the book.

"Thank you," said the girl as she made her way to her friend.

"Er, you girls local?" asked Julian, raising his voice a little.

"Yes," she said. "You?"

"Yes," said Julian.

Her friend was getting impatient, and Nick couldn't believe Julian's blatant flirting.

"Where you off to? Fancy one for the road with us?"

The girl looked at her friend, who gave a non-committal shrug.

"Sure, why not. Nastya?"

"Oh, OK then," said Nastya.

They all shuffled together on the awkward, unforgiving picnic bench.

"So, you're Nastya and you're..."

"Lisa," she said, answering Julian's question.

"Drink?" he asked in a light-hearted voice, and they proceeded to order from the waiter.

The conversation was starting to flow when Julian asked: "You OK, Nastya?"

"Yes, although I feel as if I know you from somewhere," which immediately got a hard stare from Lisa. "Either I have a massive *déjà vu* or you're famous."

"Nope... not yet anyway! but I have to say you do too – look familiar, I mean."

The other two became bystanders as Nastya and Julian tried to figure out if they did indeed know each other. They drew an unconvinced blank but thought it best to drop the subject as it was quite apparent that Lisa had earmarked Julian for herself, and Nick was getting bored as he wasn't in Lisa's line of fire.

***

"So, what's the difference between a theory and reality?" Julian asked the girls, slightly flushed after their second drink.

Anticipating that the answer was going to be bad, Lisa finally asked, "What?"

"Well, a kid asked his dad this question for his homework" continued Julian. "His dad said go ask your mum if she would sleep with the plumber for a million quid. He came back and said mother would sleep with the plumber for a million quid.

There you go, said his dad - now go ask your sister if she'd sleep with the plumber for a million quid. He said, after asking, she would. There you go, said the dad...the difference between theory and reality... in theory we're sitting on two million quid. In reality we're living with a pair of slappers."

Julian smiled hopefully.

Nick looked down at his drink, not wanting to be part of this inevitable car-crash, when the two girls suddenly laughed in a very raucous way.

Nick looked up and smiled.

It soon became noticeable to Nastya that Lisa had her hand on Julian's leg under the table and thought maybe it was time for other plans. The sunny afternoon had played its part, and the time had come for the group to move on.

They stood together in the street and worked out who was going whereas Lisa was now holding Julian's hand. Nastya took advantage of Nick's offer to give her a lift to Hammersmith and they parted as two couples, except two people were single. The river by now had partly submerged the road.

"Your friend, Julian," said Nastya as they walked off together, "you known him long?" They got into the car.

"Years."

"Where did you meet?"

"We went to school together," said Nick.

"A famous school?" asked Nastya, smiling, looking ahead at the traffic through the grubby windscreen.

"Nothing special... a *Brothers'* school, a *De La Salle* Catholic school. Brothers are pre-priests, as it were."

"St... Joseph's?" said Nastya slowly, not knowing how she knew.

Nick turned his head and looked at her.

* * *

"Nice friend," said Julian.

"Yes, Nastya's lovely. She's got a long-term boyfriend."

"She seemed to know me, or at least she thought so..."

"Yes! Odd that. Anyway, what are we going to do? I feel a little tipsy," said Lisa, diverting the conversation away from her friend, thinking that the boyfriend mention, would firmly shut down any unwanted avenues in *that* direction.

"Best take advantage of that; rule number one in the *Gentleman's Bible*," said Julian, staring into Lisa's eyes as he moved forward to kiss her on the mouth.

"Not that easy," said Lisa teasingly.

"No, I know, but I am."

"Are you?"

"No, not really, but shall we try and make *us* easier... another drink?"

"Grand plan! Jeeves, take me to my destination!" and they staggered, laughing, to the next river pub.

An hour later, the pair were decidedly 'on the way', as the night began to draw in. "Well, itsh time te make a mooove," said Julian, jokingly.

"Yesh!" reciprocated Lisa, "Tak-Shii?"

"Yesh... Where to? I live at Hampton Wick... you can drop me off on the way to yours," said Julian, a little sad that such a fun afternoon was drawing to a close. With the plan agreed, they finally arrived in the taxi outside Julian's block.

"So, I'll call you tomorrow if you want?"

"Sure," said Lisa as she got out of the cab with him.

Julian looked at her, surprised. "Aren't you going?..." he trailed off as Lisa squeezed his hand. "Oh!"

***

Recollection

Lisa weaved her way to the bathroom. When she came back to bed, she realised that the scale of her impending hangover was going to be record-breaking, even more so when she noticed the unexplained bottle of vodka next to the dressing table. Her eyes then moved to the shadows on the bed and concentrated on Julian's handsome face and dark wavy hair. He had a smile on his face in his deep sleep and she understood why. Quickly concluding that she had done the right thing, Lisa fell back into a bottomless, happy, deep sleep herself.

The smell of coffee finally stirred Julian's unexpected but welcome guest.

"How you feeling?"

"Crap, thank you," said Lisa, shakily accepting the coffee.

"I've got to go soon, I'm afraid, I have some children to look after."

"Oh, I didn't realise..." said Lisa defensively.

"Figuratively speaking. I'm referring to my builders!"

"Oh, good. You're not married, are you?"

"Nope."

"Ever before?"

"Never before."

"Oh, nor I," said Lisa, once again seeing Julian in a positive light.

"When do you have to leave? I'll get my things."

"No hurry. Chill, take your time, it's Saturday. I can meet you for lunch if you want... unless you have any other plans, of course?"

Lisa felt she should have plans but replied, "OK."

Julian calmly got his things ready to leave. "By the way," he said, "your friend, Nastya?"

"Yes?" said Lisa, clutching her half-finished coffee.

"I *do* know her. Her other half, does he have very dark skin? Like a permanent tan?"

"Yes... yes, how do you know? Did you meet?"

"We didn't meet exactly, but I saw them in a bar years ago. Her red hair and its style are pretty unforgettable. Her eyes were pretty amazing too."

"Good memory," said Lisa running her fingers through her long blonde hair. "Very pretty," she said reluctantly, "small world."

"Last night was amazing. I like you Lisa," said Julian, quickly realising that complimenting Nastya at this moment was unwise.

Taken back by his immediate warmth, she agreed with the carefully chosen word. "Likewise."

He kissed her softly, caressing one of her breasts but then suddenly pulled back. "I really must go, or there will be cement everywhere, as a truck is delivering about now."

"Who said romance isn't dead?"

"Funny, and..." Julian had to think about the double negative reply, "Can't think of an answer to that, hurting brain syndrome, I'll call about lunch, keys are in the door, just give them to me when I see you. OK?"

"OK."

"I have a spare set for me hidden out front."

"OK," said Lisa again, and the door closed. Lisa knew *exactly* where the keys were hidden. She undressed and went to take a shower. On the way back from the shower she found an old black and white school photo (unbeknown to Julian, who considered it lost) and recognised Julian in the group. She smiled and decided to keep it as a memento to be returned upon their next meeting. She happened to have a copy of *Thailand Diaries* (a travel book about Thailand, by a young couple who explored the islands), and put the photo between the pages. She had the copy to give to Nastya for her imminent travels to the country.

1993. Keys

Julian almost had a skip in his step. The builders guessed why as the cement truck finished unloading. He chatted happily to the site manager for a while but was hugely distracted at the thought of lovely Lisa padding around barefoot in his flat. He finally decided on the right moment to call about lunch without seeming desperate.

Her phone rang, but no-one answered. Odder still, there was no recorded message, and the phone just cut off. Presuming he had misdialled, he tried again, smiling at a passing builder. As he looked out at the street from a half-finished window frame, the same thing happened again. He presumed he must have taken her number down wrong and decided to head back.

"Just off for a meeting, be back in about an hour." He always gave this time frame to keep the team on their toes, so they would never really know *when* he would materialise. They, of course, knew this by now and didn't expect to see him back until the next day - putting on the kettle after he left. He walked at a quick pace across the bridge back to his flat.

Accidentally slamming the main door open and causing a loud bang, he ran down the four stairs to his front door and rang the bell.

Girls have power, he thought. *I've only known her five minutes and I'm ringing my own doorbell to be let into my own flat*. There was no reply, and he looked through the letterbox and saw no sign of life. He wondered if he'd been set up for a burglary as he went out the back to the dustbins to where the spare key was hidden. It was there. He went back to his front door. He realised she never did say where she lived in the taxi the night before.

The mortice Chubb lock was on, and upon entering he expected to see the key on the doormat, but it wasn't there. He called Lisa's name, even though he felt the flat was empty. It was quite modest with only two bedrooms and a small living room. It was cosy, clean, and homely. The decor was adequate with one or two tasteful pieces of furniture and works of art dotted around, which gave it a very middle-class 30-something bachelor feel.

He sat on a kitchen stool and tried to understand what was going on. He spotted a note in the middle of the island-style breakfast bar. 'Ah!' he said to himself and leant over to get it. A key fell out as he unfolded it. He read the short message: *I had to go; you'll understand.* It was unsigned.

"Eh?" he said out loud, bewildered.

The key. Something isn't right, he thought, and then said out loud, "Of course!" He now realised what! It was only possible to Chubb lock the front door and leave the key inside, *if* you dropped it through the letterbox because the key had to be physically turned in the lock. He questioned for a moment if the Chubb *was* on when he came back, but he was sure it was.

 He then worked out the only scenario (unless she had climbed out of windows) – *Lisa must have known where the spare key was. She must have collected it and then come in and left his key on the breakfast bar. Then retracing her steps, she must have left, locking the bottom lock with the spare on the way, and putting the emergency key back by the dustbins.*

That just didn't make any sense to him as he only by chance met her yesterday and he'd never seen her before in his life. But how did she know where the spare was? And why do that? He stood up and sat down again and then dialled out. The whole thing didn't stack up.

***

The phone rang at the other end about three times. "Hi Nick..."

"Hi buddy, SOOO, how'd it go last night? You never cease to amaze me! I'm jealous."

"So you should be," joked Julian. "I too feel pretty amazed at the moment!"

"Why, what have you done?" said Nick, fishing.

"Well, Lisa's gone, and yes, she did spend the night, and I think we made a connection..."

"Obviously!"

"Ha-ha, no, I arranged to see her for lunch and left her in my flat..." Julian went on to describe the events.

"That IS different, have you got a stalker?"

"I'll accept any theory at the moment. It looks like the whole meeting was not by chance."

"Don't be silly, you've been watching too many spy movies, mate!"

"Well, you explain then."

"I'll think on it."

"Do you have Nastya's phone number?" asked Julian.

"No."

"Shit! Do you know where they live?"

"Sorry, no," waivered Nick.

"Think she might have said that she lived in Hampton, not sure," said Julian.

***

A hunch!

Julian had lunch on his own in an old pub by Hampton Court, going over what had happened and realising it was the shortest-lived euphoria he'd ever experienced. He walked back through the ancient park, past deer and the old ladies feeding swans on ponds partly concealed by rushes. The sun was shining, and two kids cycled past, disappearing into a shady thicket of hundred-year-old oaks. The breeze soothed his mind, and he reached the high black wrought-iron fence and went through the turnstile towards his flat across the road.

He opened the door and called Lisa's name again, but she wasn't there. The sun shone through the 1930s Crittall windows in the living room and he opened two of them. He started up his computer and worked for the best part of three hours until he noticed the sun was setting. As he got up to shut the windows, an alert sounded from his computer.

This would have been unexceptional in most circumstances except he had it on silent. He looked down at his computer and bent over to click on what he presumed he should click. The screen image contorted and changed to show the message sheet. The sender was under the name of 'Chourne Gora.' The message was brief, and it simply said '22'. Just at that point, the computer shut down. He had run out of power.

"Crap!" said Julian and quickly plugged in the charger.

After a minute the homepage came up again, but this time no message.

He dialled out, hung up and immediately walked to the kitchen. He looked up to the 'odds and sods' basket kept on the top of a kitchen unit and reached in. He had a hunch which was about to be proved right.

Julian pulled out the 'along the right lines' letter from the other day and laid it out on the breakfast bar. He then deliberately placed Lisa's note next to it. Bingo! Same writing. This discovery sent a million questions and scenarios running through his head. He decided to collate them on paper and started to write.

'1. She knew who I was at pub

2. She is a good actress

3. Is she a spy?

4. Is she from the government?

5. Did she know of me all those years ago...? Yes! Must have.

6. Why did she give away her handwriting? She knew I'd put two and two together.

7. Must mean she wants me to know otherwise she would have typed?

64

8. She must be on my side.

10. The key was a clue for me knowing I'd put two and two.

9. Will...'

He couldn't think of a 9, but this was quite enough. *What a day*, he thought, as he pulled a cork out of a bottle of red opened the night before and poured some wine into an elegant glass. He then remembered Nastya. He knew her too, or at least he thought he did. He then wondered if they were both in this together. He rang Nick back.

"You really are full of surprises!" laughed Nick after Julian explained what he found out.

"Did she tell you anything about herself at all?" pressed Julian. "Did she give any clues about Lisa? Anything?"

Nick couldn't think of anything and went silent for a moment. "Nothing, sorry mate."

"Ah! Cheers for trying. I'll call you tomorrow."

"Cool."

Julian hung up and stared vacantly out of the window, holding his glass. This really was the strangest thing, he thought, looking at his reflection in the window, realising he had to act as some wheels were clearly in motion. He concluded that he would continue as normal and take heed of Lisa's original note.

He reminisced about the night before. Lisa was beautiful and he hadn't laughed like that in ages. She really made him feel alive. He decided whatever happened, if he got the chance to see her again, he wouldn't let her go so easily. He poured another glass of wine and looked around the moodily lit room which now felt empty without her. He felt stupid letting a one-night stand influence him so badly. He tried to watch some TV and realised he just wasn't into it so he went to bed wondering what tomorrow would bring.

***

Meanwhile, Nick tried hard to retrace the conversations with Nastya and remember where she headed after he dropped her off. *'There lies a clue'*, he thought. *'She headed away from the underground implying that she must know the area; Hammersmith Tube wasn't merely her transit point'.*

***

In Montenegro, the recent event that Julian had met Lisa was being monitored. Julian was completely oblivious that he was caught up in a web created by two conflicting spiders.

"He checked the gold price three times. Julian knows something."

"Thank you Reklem, we'll watch carefully." P. Bun Ma sat back in his wing back leather chair and gently put the phone down. Reklem had been tipped off to watch Lisa Engles by the computer research teams. They noticed that they were being followed by Lisa but couldn't understand who she was. Now this Julian had turned up and Reklem felt things were getting a bit out of control, especially as this was meant to be top secret. Reklem decided that some action was required and soon. She dialled out...

1993. The biggest heist the world has ever seen

Lisa had been watching Julian's research for some time now, unbeknown to him. She set him tasks which he was oblivious to by sending him mysterious internet leads prompting his research journalism into the country's gold and insurance irregularities. She put him on the right path on several occasions when he strayed and inadvertently Julian was becoming more and more of a front man for Lisa to hide behind. These leads were getting noticed by Julian, which was also Lisa's objective.

Lisa loved to have fun to the point where she could be almost dangerous, taking things to the limit was one of her traits. She was slight, blonde and a tomboy with sparkling blue eyes and a captivating smile. Her raunchy horse-like laugh surprised many. She had studied Quantum Gravity at Uni, and at 30 she had done more than most. She had adopted a very upper-class English accent along the way, which was deliberate, as she was from Australia. She realised that being described as native and 'posh' would be a way forward in her chosen society.

Lisa was now at the point where she needed to alert Julian to what he was about to discover without raising alarm bells, which by now were at a very sensitive setting. Lisa presumed that Reklem must be on to him. Lisa knew, unlike Reklem, that Julian's search was not deliberate but happened by chance and used this 'joker in the pack' to her advantage. As a result, a lot of what was going on didn't make sense to Reklem.

This mission had started when her sister Viv invited her to a party a few years ago and she spotted Julian, then a stranger, lying face down on a sofa, totally and utterly drunk. Wasted, by 11pm. Viv explained to Lisa that he was in fact a neighbour who'd half accomplished a lifetime ambition, which he explained was to crawl home drunk, literally, after a party.

"'A big tick in my box of things to do before I die,' he gurgled to me," said Viv, "before he slid down onto the sofa. My house party was the perfect opportunity, except he got too excited and peaked too early that night. Wild horses wouldn't get him back, even though the journey to his house was only a few yards across the road."

Julian had therefore actually met Lisa... except he didn't know it. Future events with Viv brought him into Lisa's line of vision. She presumed him to be an agent of some kind after studying his online research but soon found out that he was an innocent party that had stumbled upon what was to be the biggest heist the world had ever seen.

***.

1993. Julian meets Gerry

Julian was still scratching his head about Lisa. He had quickly got over the feeling of lust and was now more than curious as to who the hell she *was*. He compared his brain to those puzzles comprising sketches of animals walking up and around never-ending staircases which take you back to where you started. *Relativity* by M.C. Escher, he remembered. He felt he needed just a few more pieces of information to break through this enigmatic puzzle. But where on earth was this going to come from? Where *did* he have to search?

He walked along the river across Kingston Bridge to the river restaurants which looked up at the bridge. They were crowded, with little room to spare. But in the corner, he saw a large table which only had one customer, a large man who Julian felt had quite an imposing aura about him - which probably explained why the seats opposite him were vacant. Julian was starving and couldn't be bothered shopping around, so he decided to try and share the table. The man looked up from his newspaper and Julian asked if he wouldn't mind him sharing his six-seater table.

"Be my guest," said the man, who stared deep into Julian's eyes.

Julian sat a while before he could order. The waiter left and Julian caught the man's eye. The man nodded and smiled.

"Hi, nice day," said Julian awkwardly.

"It is," said the man, adding little else to encourage conversation.

"Julian. Nice to meet you." He leant over to shake the man's hand.

"Gerry. Likewise." and the man smiled.

The smile of an executioner thought Julian as both sat for a while before speaking any further. They caught each other's eye again and smiled once more.

"You from around here?" asked Julian looking around.

"No, just visiting. I live in Chelsea – seeing relatives."

"Oh, I know Flood Street, Chelsea, it's where Thatcher had a house."

"I actually live by the river, other end," said Gerry calmly.

"Maybe I know you, I've eaten at *Foxtrot Oscars* often, that's right outside Cheyne Court's entrance."

"It is, it is," and Gerry looked a little harder at Julian.

"I don't know about you, but I need an afternoon beer," said Julian looking equally inquisitively at his new acquaintance. "They're the best in my opinion."

"Agreed, I'll join you if you don't mind?" said Gerry.

Julian had anticipated this answer after he had pre-judged the man's large reddish nose. "Be my guest, I feel as if I need – no – *deserve* one."

"Oh dear, sounds like there's a woman involved," commented Gerry, looking up at Julian. "You youngsters always worry too much."

"Very astute," replied Julian, "and on the money."

"There's more to life than girls, I found. I took up sailing. It was less stressful being in a force 10 on the Bay of Biscay." He gave a wry smile.

"I believe this one is special," defended Julian.

"They all are." And the conversation broke off to catch the attention of the uninterested waiter who was circling nearby aimlessly.

They finally ordered from the waiter who (Julian figured) had majored in the 'looking anywhere but at the customer' school of waitering. The al-fresco restaurant was still busy.

"If I had a restaurant, I'd give each customer a cattle prod to encourage service," said Gerry.

"Or a catapult," Julian added. "Or an electrode fitted to their butt with an engaging button on each table. The more you pressed, the greater the voltage – the higher the jump."

"Ha-ha yes," Gerry said loudly, "that *would* equate to service."

"Probably not so much of a smile, mind," cut in Julian using his best Geordie accent.

They laughed again.

"What would be his tip?" asked Julian.

"Anti-afro hair gel!"

They both pointed at each other in acknowledgement to the statement and smirked.

"The restaurant is probably so tight they'd dock his electricity electrocution bill off his wages," said Julian, laughing.

They paused and pulled themselves together then Gerry continued, "So, adding to your life's pint miles to make up for this lass, are you?"

"Pint miles?" questioned Julian, grinning, knowing this to be some sort of intro. He figured Gerry had had a few beers before this encounter, judging by his flamboyant manner, which didn't seem to tally with what he imagined to be a tough personality.

"Yes, I once measured how much drink I had in my life, and decided the base of a pint glass could be used as a medium for measurement. Each pint you drink is one beer glass base. Put them together and you get about 5 bases in a foot. Multiply that and you end up with how many miles you've drunk," explained Gerry with a deadpan face.

Julian laughed. "So how many miles have you drunk?"

"Four and a half."

"Epic," said Julian, trying immediately to work out his life's tally, "I'll have to get back to you about mine."

"How do you know Flood Street so well?" enquired Gerry.

"I was dying to tell you before we got distracted. I used to know an alcoholic who lived in Cheyney Court. He knew…"

"George Best," interrupted Gerry.

"YES, yes!" said Julian, adjusting his voice tone, "how on earth do you know that?"

"Bet it was Peter?

"Er."

"I bought his flat from probate when he passed away – bless his soul."

"That's ridiculous," said Julian, "what a small world! It *was* Peter." He paused and continued a little taken aback, "He did have good taste in women you know – he always rented his three bedrooms to young girls. I dated one of them. That's how I know him. You'll know which bedroom I had the most fun in I guess?"

"Which one, tell me. I hope it doesn't force a sale!" quipped Gerry.

"The one overlooking the entrance courtyard. The big one."

"Oh no, that's my bedroom!"

"Shit, sorry!"

"Always someone there before you in life. No hidden used condoms I should know about is there?" joked Gerry.

"No… no, no, no." Replied Julian, deliberately being unconvincing.

"Doesn't really matter, I'll leave that to the new owner to discover – I sold the flat recently."

"For a good price, I'm sure. Do you know, I think I do know you; did you drink at the *Phoenix Arms* around the corner where..."

"George Best drank, yes."

"Hmm," said Julian, "small world indeed. Ridiculously small. You're not my Dad, are you?" he joked.

"Cheeky bugger," replied Gerry and they both ordered another beer to add to their 'pint miles'.

✳✳✳

"Ah, here's the family," and Gerry chugged down his pint slamming his beer glass down on the table. "It's been an extraordinary hour; I won't be thanked for my breath by my daughter. We must meet again sometime. Here's my card and maybe a clue as to why you think you know me."

Julian took the card as he stood up, and they shook hands. He glanced down at the card and paused - it read *Gerry Absalom, MP*.

1993. Lisa knows Gerry?

Gerry Absalom, MP, thought Julian. "Fancy that, an MP," he said to himself. He looked up at the river and tried to catch a waiter's eye for the bill.

If he had looked harder, he would have seen Lisa in the next restaurant who was watching him. It was very risky as Gerry was a potential danger to her as she wasn't quite sure yet, on which side of the fence Gerry sat.

Julian left the waiter a tip and decided to head back home. He still couldn't get Lisa out of his mind. He turned the key to open the door to his apartment after his short walk. As he closed the door behind him and looked down, there was another note. He unfolded it. It was Lisa's writing and read, *Be patient xx. I think Gerry's dangerous.*

"What the fuck," Julian said out loud to himself and immediately opened the door and knocked on the door opposite. Mark, the neighbour, eventually answered and Julian asked if he had seen a girl hanging around. Mark replied in the negative and Julian ran outside. Confused, Mark closed his door. Julian stood awhile with his hands on his hips, perplexed at what was happening. This confirmed in his mind that he was being followed.

But why? he thought.

There was a huge upside to this note, Julian concluded, and that was that Lisa was interested, even though she seemed to be like a shadow he couldn't see. Subconsciously he started to piece together the time they had shared. Knowing where his keys were was a big one. Was the Swan meeting a chance meeting? She knew about Gerry so she must have been following for a while. Was she watching him now? He glanced out the window.

He then realised something new... she knew Gerry. That put his mind into overdrive as it meant that the Gerry meeting was not by chance either although *he* had sought out Gerry's table. *So how could this be? The other view could be that Lisa was following and the Gerry meeting was a coincidence. But the note negated this. The whole scenario was literally fantastic.*

He then remembered the first note: *You were on the right lines.* This he could relate to, as it referred to his investigation. He then considered Gerry to be a possible focus of further investigation. "I've got to do something," he said out loud. "Gerry, who are you?"

***

The next day Julian started with a purpose. After his daily meeting with the builders, he went down to his old office at the Richmond Times. A couple of old faces were there – they were pleased to see him, but they only had a brief chat as everyone was busy. He asked if he could have access to his old files, which was granted, and he was shown a desk he could operate from.

Before he started, he remembered that Lisa had been with Nastya and Nick had left her at Hammersmith where the trail went cold. He had so many questions that Lisa could answer. He felt she was about to come into his life once again soon. *The sooner the better,* he hoped.

He flipped open the computer and put his old password in. There was the old information about the insurance investigation. Immediately he noticed that there was something different about the information. The name of a past presumed link in Laos had been deleted in a way that would not have been noticed by other eyes. Someone had made a number of small deletions. This now shook out Julian's lethargy towards the case and, coupled with recent events and Lisa's note, confirmed that somebody was nervous about his findings.

It's time to get the magnifying glass out and find out what somebody was so afraid of. Whatever it is, is there to be found, then I'll know if I'm the Queen or the pawn in this chess game.

1993. Lisa's Road heads East

One evening Lisa was reflecting on her father's death and how his body had been discovered on his yacht by the Chinese port authorities. They had found it adrift off the mainland, with her father slumped at the foot of the stairs, dead. The report said he must have fallen down the gangway during a storm, breaking his neck. Lisa didn't believe this for one minute as the jenny (forward sail) was still unfurled with the mainsail partly reefed, which she knew was not storm rigging. So the authorities had clearly lied.

Her father was a diplomat for the British in the 80s and mentioned to her in veiled messages that something was up. He later sent her some photos of his yacht on a night sail with the moon gleaming above in a clear sky - illuminating the Jeanneau's full white sails during a beam reach (the best point of sail with the wind giving maximum push). Her father wrote on the back that this was his fourth day at sea. Lisa thought it strange that he sent photos of the boat which didn't even feature himself.

This, for no particular reason, now played on her mind. Then she realised that something didn't add up, they shouldn't have appeared in the photo at all! The fenders being out along the side of the boat in the photo was a message. Being a sailor herself she knew the first thing you do after you cast off is to take the fenders in, yet the message said this was day four at sea so why on earth were the fenders still out?

For a hugely seasoned yacht master, this didn't stack up at all and Lisa, as intended, realised this – her father knew she would. Prying eyes were unlikely to spot this deliberate mistake, unless someone was of nautical stock. It was a puzzle.

(Her ensuing journey to China yielded nothing and confirmed the conspiracy. She faced a brick wall with no one knowing anything except his secretary who mentioned that she should be wary of a man called Gerry. She took heed and left, frustrated at her lack of progress).

Lisa worked in banking, setting up high profile accounts for companies as big as BP. She worked in an office next to the OXO Tower restaurant on the Thames River embankment. After Lisa returned from the fruitless foray into China, she once again stared at the photo with the fenders. The message on the back which she'd read a thousand times, said *Day 4 at sea, Lady M. 389 14 1.*

She had never worked out what the numbers were but presumed them to be something to do with a registration or insurance number for the yacht which led to the obvious question: *Why* put *that in?* She thought it to be a possible bank sort code which she tried to locate on the boat register, but to no avail.

She now had a new idea! She messed around on the computer screen by putting the alphabet underneath the numbers which meant that the number 3 came in line with the letter C. She continued and got CHIADA.

Who or what on earth is Chiada? She checked the dictionary and got nothing. She thought maybe it could be the name of a person, possibly *M Chiada*. She put that down as a possibility to be checked later. Still her mind told her to explore other avenues while she was at it. So she did the same process except backwards – *Adaihc* – then with an M. Still nothing! Just another name to check!

She got up, walked around, and made a cup of tea. Glancing sideways at the computer screen, still standing up and sipping from her cup, she realised something that should have been obvious to her from the start. It was 389 14 1. There was the number 14, not 1 and 4. She eagerly revisited the alphabet and the 14 equated to the letter 'N'. "Bingo", she said out loud. "China...its China. Yessss!"

She typed in *China 389141* and got nothing. She then typed *CHINA 389141* and the screen went mad.

She put her cup down and focused on the screen, which illuminated her profile in the dimly lit room. Her pupils dilated to take in the odd information displayed on the screen. It had information on three vaults, one of which was in Koh Samui, Thailand. *Fancy that*, she thought. Montenegro and London were the others.

There were code numbers comprising numerals and numbers. But what really caught her eye were names, placed under each country. P. Bun Ma and P. Payam, Angela Reklem and Charles De Vere and Gerry Absalom respectively. A whole load more account numbers then started to scroll down. There were lists of European ministers' names, some of which she recognised. She took a screenshot immediately of the first page and scrolled down when suddenly the screen went blank. Someone was onto her and shut her down. They knew she'd seen what she'd seen. She got the screenshot up and took a photograph.

The rest of her evening was spent looking over her shoulder whilst destroying the hard drive to the computer. She now knew who 'they' were and that this was big!

During further investigation into *CHINA 389141* Lisa became aware of a young journalist called Julian. His name had come up after he began enquiring about the country's gold supplies and its relation to money printing. The question he asked which had no answers, was, who's seen the gold and who is responsible for its record keeping.

She saw that Julian approached some leading political figures who agreed to see him because they weren't sure what he knew – upon understanding he understood nothing – they fobbed him off. He mentioned to them about a person called Reklem who seemed to be a major instigator of gold transactions. It was hard for Lisa not to see the lengths to which the ministers tried to deflect from the question.

She also noted his newspaper articles questioning why insurance was necessary, as the only people who seemed to benefit were Chinese manufacturing companies - who lobbied European politicians to make insurance law. Julian was trying to correlate a connection between high-cost European goods influenced by high insurance, to cheaply manufactured Chinese goods which had no insurances involved.

Lisa wasn't sure if Julian was a player/undercover agent, or a simple journalist who'd discovered the link by chance. If he wasn't innocent in his research, then Lisa knew it was only a matter of time before he would 'disappear'. The clock started to countdown when Lisa realised that people *were* on Julians trail.

After further investigations Lisa had discovered that the gold was slowly but steadily being relocated - from *all* European countries. She was staggered at the cunning and the sheer size of 'theft' and was alarmed by the prospects of what would happen to society upon its realisation.

Thereafter she spent all her hours making sure she remained undetected whilst following the perpetrators, hoping to eventually release her findings to parties that would act in their national interests. The last part of her plan was proving especially hard as almost everyone seemed corruptible. She also picked up that politicians with no families were the ones mainly involved in the plot, as they could vanish without consequences to family members when things got *hot*.

Her mission was compromised when from afar, she fell in love with Julian.

So, she wrote him a note.

1993. Trust and Timm

Lisa had found backup, which she needed, as the pressure was becoming unbearable. Anyone she knew or met could be her assassin. She decided she was going to take a chance on a patriotic, God-fearing, English MP called Paul Timmingham. She *felt* his natural honesty, and knew he was concerned at the level of influence money was having on his colleagues - to the point where he could no longer associate with them. He also wondered about the source and motives of their corruption.

Lisa first met Timmingham at a drinks party in Chelsea on Royal Hospital Road at a place called Foxtrot Oscars. She picked up his distrust of Gerry Absalom MP at this gathering. Paul and Lisa spoke to each other at length at the party and kept in touch thereafter, to the point where Lisa considered him a confidant, finally telling him of the plot she called the *Siam Conspiracy*.

It was a risky thing for her to do, based on a hunch, but she got lucky. Paul turned out to be to be the Right Honourable Gentleman in every sense and disclosed that he too was aware of the conspiracy, although, he was not as informed as Lisa. She was stunned to realise that she was not alone and was thankful that Paul was very influential, both at home and abroad, knowing the 'right people'. Lisa, in Paul, had finally found some armour in which to protect herself. She could now go on the offensive.

Lisa showed Paul what was going on and requested a wage in the millions as a consultancy fee, plus anonymity, to save the West's assets. Compared to the billions involved, Paul considered her fee a small price to pay, as she was also putting her life on the line.

Paul was unsure of Lisa's intentions but decided that doing nothing was not an option as she possessed valuable information. He also understood that *his* life was now on the line – being a confirmed link. He had seen the trail of death that followed the *Siam Conspiracy* which rendered life as cheap. So, the secret remained between Lisa and Paul, who could provide international backup as required when the trigger was pulled.

Lisa was now the trigger.

***

The Third Handshake

1978. Laos.

Angela Reklem was sweating and nervous, seated in a heavy, antiquated train, infested by cockroaches. The powerful old locomotive was ploughing its way through the northern Thai jungle and its central plains. In total isolation, it weaved its way across endless palm-covered land, broken up by flat, bright green paddy fields. Occasionally, slow-moving rivers appeared and disappeared under rusting bridges that supported the line as the train rumbled on.

It was ferociously humid, which was a problem to Reklem as she was more used to the East German snow than this heat. She stared through the rust-stained window and wondered what lay ahead, as this was as far away from her comfort zone as she could get. Westerners like her were a rarity because of the recent Vietnam war, so she was more than nervous of the men sitting around her.

Reklem's eye was continually caught by a large man sat in another seat two rows in front of her. He was watching her and the other passengers carefully. His name was Henrick, Reklem's designated bodyguard and his size stood out amongst the shorter locals.

He offered her little comfort as Reklem knew size was shown to mean very little in the Vietnamese/American conflict. The Far-Eastern men had no fear and combined with unfathomable wiry strength, they had an air of invincibility. Still, the men on the carriage kept at arm's length, confused at what she was doing there. To them, it was like coming across a brand-new Mercedes, parked in a dangerous neighbourhood – unlocked. You dare not touch it as the owner is probably someone who didn't need to lock *anything*. The menace was more than a match for any security system.

Reklem was on her way to cross the mighty Mekong River and onto Vientiane, Laos, which lay on its banks. In years to come this exact route would become a major visa run destination and the same carriages of the train would be full of young happy twenty-something backpackers, talking about their adventures in Thailand. Reklem feared this journey could be part of a set-up and was dreading this border crossing.

Reklem was an unassuming agent for the USSR, being short, fiercely intelligent and slightly overweight from stodgy Soviet cooking. Today she chose to dress in khaki, being influenced by films she'd seen about Westerners in the Far East. Her replication was so exact she almost looked like a film extra.

A Chinese girl made her way down the aisle and sat next to Reklem, which seemed strange to her as there were empty seats in front. This annoyed Reklem, who briefly broke away from her observation of the foreign countryside to check out the new passenger. She figured the girl was in her twenties, roughly the same age as Reklem. The Chinese girl sat neatly and didn't alter her forward gaze, relying on her peripheral vision to check out Reklem. There was an hour or so left of the six-hour journey and neither passenger altered their stance once until they approached the terminal. Reklem wondered what she was up to.

The train finally slowed, only to speed up again, jolting and unbalancing the passengers. Fighting the train's force of forward momentum, it finally ground to a halt. A momentary silence ensued, followed by some locals jumping off. Reklem looked around, taking care not to make eye contact with the girl sitting stiffly next to her.

The girl then changed seats and sat opposite, giving Reklem a brief smile to which Reklem, relieved, cracked a smile back. The train started to move slowly once more toward the station platform a short distance ahead. The station seemed tiny against an immense grey sky above and behind. Blue signs written in Thai, confirmed the destination and the end of Reklem's journey.

This was it, Reklem thought, and reconfirmed to herself that she wasn't going to be afraid – *What's going to be, is to be* she thought – as there was now no turning back. After a slow entry to the station platform, the train stopped, and the passengers impatiently got off. The Chinese girl was not in a hurry and remained rooted to her seat until the train was empty, barring the three strangers. Reklem stood up.

"We had better get off now," said the girl in broken German, which took Reklem a little by surprise. She looked at her bodyguard Henrick, who raised his eyebrows without a smile and got up.

"Shall we?" said the Chinese girl, gesturing toward the door. Reklem nodded her head, saying nothing, and they made their way off the carriage, carefully navigating the long drop to the low platform. Despite having huge Henrick to protect her against this tiny girl, Reklem still felt very naked.

There was a queue ahead at the border control, predominantly made up of local Laotians who were returning from their toils in the Thai paddy fields. Reklem now became acutely aware how short everyone was, as at home she was not the tallest - but here was a different story, she felt tall! The queue diminished rapidly, and she was left with the border guards who didn't seem phased by this

Westerner and her large companion with German passports. She was ready for an unpleasant strip search and for Henrick to be set upon by dogs and police, but, nothing! They waved her through, smiling politely as they passed. This made her even more uneasy; it was as if everybody had been briefed about their arrival.

She found herself in a large empty square, surrounded by nothing except views of the immensely wide river beyond the border buildings. She could see all the way up and down the banks, which had a dirt road running along it with no traffic – just the odd peasant riding a bike. Reklem assumed an exotic sculpted sandstone archway about two hundred metres away on the left was the entrance to the town. She summoned Henrick to follow, and they walked quickly as dusk was upon them. Reklem's superiors had told her she would be met by someone at the first temple past the entrance. The Chinese girl appeared again and joined them on the walk. *So, she's the one,* thought Reklem, nodding her head.

Reklem passed two huge stone carvings of elephants, which made up part of the impressive archway to the small town. The town, in Reklem's eyes, looked like a film set depicting the Dark Ages, where the only sources of light were oil lamps, fires and candles. Silhouetted people wandered around wide, dusty streets lined with single storey shacks, blanketed by the heat and humidity. The steely blue sky above was darkening fast and roosting birds hovered over tree canopies in urgent search for a branch to spend the night.

Dodging the odd cart, the three continued in silence through a maze of exotic statues of giant Buddhas, dragons and other mystical storybook figures. Reklem presumed this area was about appreciation of the gods and the mystical powers that might decide the local people's destiny.

"I am 'A'," said the Chinese girl, finally breaking her silence. "You are Reklem," she stated without emotion.

"Yes," replied Reklem.

"We have an appointment ... we are not far. You are safe."

1978. Plan A

They arrived at an old wooden colonial building, which was probably built by the French. It was a beautiful structure with two wooden dragons protecting the entrance door. As they approached, the doors opened unprompted, and they passed two men dressed in white gowns facing each other in the hall. Even though the guards stood to attention, motionless and in silence, Reklem could still feel their eyes following their every move. They made their way into a low-ceilinged palatial room where two men (she presumed to be Chinese or Vietnamese), sat behind a large mahogany table. Only rotating fans broke the silence in the dimly lit room.

"Your friend must come with me," said A, and she gestured with her head to Reklem's bodyguard to follow her back out of the room.

As they left, the double doors closed. Reklem accepted the men's request to sit opposite them at the table. "Good evening, Reklem, we have been intrigued to meet you".

"Likewise," she responded edgily.

"I am P. Bun Ma, and this is P. Panya. We have been in contact with you for a while now, and we have an operation we believe that you are interested in?"

Reklem knew that 'P' was a title given to someone high up in Thai society, just as 'Khun' was the same as 'Mister'.

She bowed her head slightly and said, "Yes, I am." She sipped jasmine tea with a tiny white flower floating on the surface, which had been pre-prepared and positioned in front of where she sat.

"We share similar views." added P. Bun Ma.

"The West. You have informed me that you have an idea on how to stop their advance?" said Reklem.

"We do, and following our information, we believe you should be the person in charge."

"Who was your contact in Germany?" Reklem asked, fishing.

P. Panya smiled and stared at Reklem. There was a momentary silence between the three.

P. Bun Ma broke the silence. "Before we start, make no mistake, if you betray us, we have serious ways of correcting the position. It's something I have to say. I'm sure you understand."

Taken aback by P. Bun Ma's immediate threat and direct approach, Reklem adjusted her position on her chair. "I understand."

P. Panya spoke. "We have decided, after Vietnam, further military engagement with the West is futile. They are too organised. So, through teachers we are establishing allies of the future. We own the teachers, so soon the West's children's minds will belong to us. We also have a second line of attack."

"Which is?" asked Reklem, leaning forward.

"Treason."

Reklem wasn't ready for such a basic answer and sat back. She thought of several responses thereafter, but none settled. Her thoughts were interrupted by P. Bun Ma.

"Treason, or an act of it, against a state or country is unacceptable.

Yes?"

"Yes."

"It's the only thing that keeps politicians in line. To act against your own people is unacceptable... it would be treasonous. Now imagine if treason were no longer a crime."

"And how would you get to that point?"

"Take away the country..."

Reklem smiled, confused, slightly deflated and like a teenager (who'd earlier asked for money - agreed to by the parents), being told over dinner that the best way to get money is to get a job. Reklem decided she had come this far, so it was best to hear them out.

"Take away the country. Blow it up?" Said Reklem with an air of sarcasm.

"Dilute it. Make people angry. The day the population won't want to pay tax or even fight for it, is when treason is no longer considered a crime."

"Ok, you got me. How do I do that?"

"Disarm the borders. Lose them. If Ho Chi Mihn had had no borders, no North or South Vietnam...no Laos, no China, then who would he have been fighting? Who would he have been fighting for? *What* would he have been fighting exactly?"

"Good point."

"We need the West to be lulled into lethargy. Let them take their borders for granted to a point where they won't fight. Their memory of war in their comfortable life will soon be forgotten. They will however, fight for money."

"And religion," interrupted P. Panya

"Noted," said Bun Ma. "The West is in love with money. Money is a substitute for something that doesn't exist - wealth! And like water, wind and fire, it is extremely destructive, except it slips through your hands when you try to hold on to it.

The thing is *politicians* print money. Print the imaginary wealth - and without treason they too can be bought. There is nothing stopping influence on politicians who operate without guilt. The few that are loyal to a country they *'used'* to have will be few, and again everyone has their price.

"So, we buy politicians, then what?"

"They give us their gold after we threaten them with blackmail. Sex, prostitutes, difficult situations, greed... are far more destructive than bombs or bullets. We have a secret weapon too. Home computers are coming soon, which gives access to home pornography. They will naturally watch it but unbeknown to them these sites will relay to us exactly what they are watching. We will know every perverted request they make. I need say no more on that point.

Politicians, in my opinion are attention seekers with little or no confidence, no self-esteem. Generally, they've never run anything or made anything, so they need an alter ego. They'd ideally be pop stars if they could, but honestly, they're too ugly. How many pin-up politicians do you know?" Bun Ma paused, "... exactly!"

Reklem smiled at the last points, now fully understanding that they had an unreserved hatred for 'soft' greedy Western leaders.

"So, not only will they sell the family silver to avoid bad publicity if caught, but also the country's gold.

Have you ever seen anyone's gold reserves?" asked P. Bun Ma ignoring her smile.

"No."

"Nor have I. So, if it goes missing who's to know? How can you miss something you've never seen? The only people to have access to it are?..."

"Politicians," replied Reklem, beginning to get the picture.

"Without fear of treason," added P. Panya.

"I see."

"...And there Reklem, is your mission," continued P. Bun Ma.

"We already have *acquired* many politicians across many countries who will do what we ask - they just need guidance. They need to know where to send the gold."

"That makes sense."

"The reward for you would make more sense than you could ever dream of."

It all seemed a little crazy to Reklem, but it added up, as she understood the reliance of people on their governments, leaving the populations and politicians vulnerable to influence - which she now understood would be the East, in disguise.

"Coming back to religion... that is the fly in the ointment. We have yet to work out a plan for that entity," interjected P. Panya, and the two men looked at each other.

"We have someone you must meet," announced Bun Ma. "Gerry."

"Gerry," repeated Reklem.

1978. Over the South China Sea

Reklem was looking down at the Chao Phraya River's many tributaries that entered the South China Sea. She was on a small four-seater, single-prop aeroplane being piloted by two men. The sea reclaimed its turquoise colour from the muddy river's deposits after a short while and the sun shone brightly down with a few clouds dotted in the distance. She had left Laos the day after the meeting and returned to Bangkok, where she boarded the plane she was now on.

She was on her own for this trip, on her way to an island off the south coast of Thailand called Koh Samui. Henrick had returned to East Germany. She went over in her mind the conversation and ideas from the previous evening. It was a plan that involved a lot of manpower and research. The plan already seemed to be in action, and she understood herself to be one of the final cogs in the machine. No more was added to the plan after the men suggested a rendezvous with Gerry, whom she was now going to see. The journey took about two hours, and the plane landed on a tiny runway in the jungle close to the coast. The pilots wai'd as she left.

Her bags were handed to her on the runway by a small Thai man who escorted her through the mainly empty building where Gerry waited in a jeep. On this short journey she realised that not a word had been spoken by the Thai men on the plane.

A tall young Englishman got out of the jeep and held out his hand, "Gerry, pleased to meet you."

The jeep was probably one of the few vehicles that could navigate the uneven, muddy road carved through the otherwise impenetrable jungle. After the recent monsoon rains, sections of the road were now on the verge of disappearing completely.

"I hear you're from East Germany," said Gerry, in his refined accent - as he held on tightly to a steering wheel that seemed to have a mind of its own due to the irregular road surface. "Have you been here before?".

"No," said Reklem, sweating profusely in the humidity, which became unbearable when sunlight shone like laser beams through the broken overhead canopy. They spoke little after that as Gerry's concentration was focused on not running the vehicle off the road. Finally, the jungle cleared, and the road ran along a beautiful shallow beach that the locals called Chaweng. There were one or two bamboo shacks, but little else of human presence to obscure this beautiful wilderness. They drove a while in comfort and passed a huge lake. Gerry had noticed that his passenger had relaxed as she looked around in awe. "It's a bit different to Germany, I suppose," said Gerry, interrupting her thoughts with a knowing smile.

"It is ... it is," said Reklem wistfully. She then did something out of character and threw her arms in the air, looking at the sky and shouting, "God, this is wonderful."

This was the last Gerry was to see of the little girl who hid behind Reklem's stoic facade. Smiling in East Germany, in the snow, during the Cold War was a rarity, as hunger was no laughing matter. Often, her family were left with nothing more than boiled potato skins to eat, and clothes were hand-me-downs. Reklem understood the meaning of poverty.

Watching the West have a ball, wanting for nothing, created great resentment within Reklem. Occasionally pop bands would play on the Western side of the Berlin Wall, thinking they were being nice to let the deprived East have a taste of how good life could be. This went down well with some but rubbed salt into the wounds of people like Reklem.

Her favourite expression was "A fat man and a starving man sitting on a park bench have nothing to say to each other". The West's exuberance, fake compassion and obliviousness to desperate need, was a strong driving force for Reklem. It was time to turn the tables on Earths smug Western rulers and show them the other side of life.

The jungle road weaved and once again ran along a beach.

"They call this Bang Rak," said Gerry, breaking the ice. "My home is up the hill over there." He turned at a fork in the road forged from red mud to go up a steep hill. After a short while there was a clearing, and Gerry said, "We're here. You see those five trees in the distance … well, the tallest one behind, I call 'Gerry'. You can see it from afar." He turned and smiled at Reklem, who reciprocated. "Good landmark if you get lost," he said, gearing down.

And there it was – isolated and magnificent – the walled house. Inside the parameter were beautiful Thai wooden buildings. Two servants dressed in white closed the wall gates after they had passed through, and another servant scurried from the main house to greet them and open the jeep doors.

Two other servants joined them to get Reklem's luggage, and they went over a small wooden bridge into the main house. "Your rooms are behind, in a separate building. Would you like some tea after you've freshened up?" asked Gerry.

Reklem nodded and smiled. "That would be very nice, thank you." She followed a servant with her bags. Gerry returned to the wooden terrace overlooking a large pond and waited, sitting on an ornately carved wooden bench, listening to the silence in the heat.

Reklem emerged after a short while and sat adjacent to Gerry, admiring the jungle mountains in the distance from the raised terrace.

"I understand you know a bit about me from P. Panya and P. Bun Ma," said Gerry, stirring his tea after adding a little sugar with an expensive-looking silver spoon.

Reklem was struck by Gerry's incredible English accent, which she thought sounded almost, she paused, and said, "Foreign," out loud with a smirk.

"Sorry, Reklem, what was that?"

"Nothing, nothing … call me Angela if you wish."

"What a lovely name. Was my mother's too, wouldn't you know." said Gerry, "Sandwich?"

Gerry looked no more than his mid-twenties in Reklem's estimation, and she thought him deceptively handsome with his mousy blonde hair and freckles. He was much taller than her and must have seemed a giant to the Thais, she thought. His love of life shone through, but she sensed a darkness lurking beneath his pleasant exterior.

"They didn't tell me much about you. I presumed you would be older," said Reklem, "judging by their portrayal of your wisdom," she added, so as not to offend.

"You're a junior politician, as was your father, who was apparently involved in the Vietnam conflict, I hear."

"Spot on. Any more?" said Gerry, leaning forward.

"The British Government let your father down and he ended up as a political prisoner in South Vietnam. He tried to persuade the West to join the North Vietnamese in the conflict. He was a friend of Ho Chi Minh.

He found out Ho Chi Minh, ironically, was actually very pro-American and lived in the States a while but somehow ended up fighting a patriotic war in his beloved Vietnam. Ho Chi Mihn thought the Americans were his allies, but they foolishly supported the French, who, as usual, made a disaster of their colonisation. If the Americans weren't such poodles, imagine the result? Vietnam would be pro-West with no war."

"An extraordinary analogy," said Gerry.

"It's not a regular supposition but I can see where it's coming from," replied Reklem.

"They killed my father, you know," said Gerry unexpectedly.

"Who?" asked Reklem, unsure of Gerry's comment.

"The West. Made me realise what an unpleasant lot we have in power. Obsessed with money and nice addresses, turning over anyone, my father for example, who could have benefited them *and* with no conscience. It's a disgusting land grab by suits," Gerry said calmly. "They're no worse than the tribes around here except they wear a tie. Not impressed! Anyway, you didn't come all this way to hear me rant. I want to show the establishment how to behave and reinstate the backbone. I have a few people in mind to start with. I believe you have similar views, and my parliamentary profile is of use to us all."

"Yes, it is," replied Reklem, realising his inexperience and anger, plus his position, made him very useful indeed.

1978. Gold!

The next day, Reklem walked along the beach with Gerry, and they discussed with enthusiasm P. Bun Ma and P. Panya's plans along with their own ideas. They were harmonious in their objectives, realising passion and not money was their motivation. The doubts about what they called the 'Siam Conspiracy' were discussed and put to one side. It was the right time to act and start the ball rolling, regardless of any flaws. Despite this, Reklem still had reservations about Gerry's true motives.

The early morning sun became uncomfortable, and they took refuge at a small, shaded beach bar made from driftwood - positioned in front of a palm plantation bordering the beach.

"There's quite a bit more to the plan than they told you ... at least you seem to think what they've told you, is all there is?" enquired Gerry.

"What do you mean?"

"Did they mention the gold?"

"Gold?" asked Reklem, turning her head away from the beautiful scenery to stare at Gerry. "They mentioned it, but in no detail."

"Oh! I'm not sure I'm at liberty to tell you." And Gerry paused to question himself. He chose to continue. "I'm sure they were going to tell you anyway, so here goes. The ultimate plan is to steal the world's gold!"

Reklem laughed out loud and then stopped. "Right! Are you trying to be funny with your English humour?" she said seriously. "I'm not here for funny stories."

Taken aback by Reklem's instant change of mood, Gerry assured her this was no joke. He went on to explain, realising Reklem was quite a bitter character.

"Actually yes, they did tell me, but I wanted to see your reaction...go on."

Gerry didn't know how to take her response but chose to continue, "Fort Knox, have you ever seen its gold? Do you know how many people have seen it? ... Three apparently!".

"The question is, is it there at all? It's impossible to get in. Only presidents have seen it, or have they?".

"What are you getting at?" asked Reklem, slightly impatiently.

"So, if the gold disappeared, no one would know, true?"

"Yes, that point was mentioned to me in Laos."

"The thing is," continued Gerry, "that no one saw it going *in*. Our research proves this. So where is it? Did it go in at all? Did all of it go in? Who was counting?"

Reklem was hooked.

"We know where the majority of the gold is, as crooked 'counters' left a trail to its unintended destination. A lot of people from both sides died finding out where the destinations were, but that's another story. Now here's the cream on the cake," continued Gerry pedantically, "we *also* know where most of the European gold is. Every country has its secret place which, again ... we know. Finding out was a long painful process spanning many years since World War Two. So, here too, we have the same situation. Lots of gold, but all relatively unseen."

Reklem was bursting with questions about how you move thousands of tonnes of gold unnoticed. Being a German communist, she refrained from using sarcasm when she finally asked, "Do you have keys to these vaults? If you do, how on earth do you propose to move it? More to the point … where to?"

"We don't have to move it all at once," said Gerry, catching the eye of the waiter lying in his hammock.

1978. The Lost Future

Reklem and Gerry ordered another coffee from the sleepy beach bar waiter.

"What I'm about to tell you is going to blow your mind. It may seem like another story or plan but it's not!" said Gerry.

Reklem now saw another side of Gerry. He was no fool, but a fiercely intelligent and passionate man. He was no different from Pol Pot except he had an English accent and dressed in a flamboyant Western way. She decided to take him seriously. She continued to listen, but didn't expect to hear what came next.

"Firstly. Archimedes invented something long ago. It got lost. His discovery was lost. He'd basically discovered the binary code that is the foundation of today's computers. If it were not lost, we'd be centuries ahead in computers. Can you imagine home computers invented three hundred years ago?"

Reklem didn't understand what a home computer was!

"I won't bore you with any more detail, but bottom line, it's been found by our people."

"I really don't follow this at all," interjected Reklem.

"Please bear with me. The connection is almost there."

"OK," said Reklem, struggling with the information and especially the heat.

"The West is advancing computers, but we are ten years ahead. They don't know this. Soon we will be able to project images on small personal screens."

Reklem was having a hard time with this jigsaw, but added, "This was mentioned in Laos."

Noticing her impatience, but unbothered, Gerry pressed on. "The key to the gold is not a physical key."

Then what is it, for god's sake? thought Reklem. Once more, the answer was unexpected.

Gerry looked at Reklem and waited for her startled reaction as he said, "Pornography!" The waves continued to break on the white sand beach as they both sat in silence. "Pornography is the key," Gerry repeated.

He's mad, thought Reklem. This whole thing is mad. This is …

"You think you're wasting your time, Angela, but trust me, you're not. I'm not mad." Reklem's eyes widened at his intuition.

"Sex is man's weakness. Men, including me, love sex. Cleopatra understood that. Most of the world's power lies with men."

This statement grated but didn't annoy Reklem, but it made her readjust on the chair, something she noticed that had been happening a lot lately.

"Blackmail was invented for sex. The forbidden fruit means secrets, secrets that some may not wish to be public knowledge under *any* circumstances. Embarrassment is a very strong yet vulnerable emotion, and it can be used.

If a politician or even a prime minister should watch perverted pornography on his private computer, do you think he'd run home and tell his wife or the country? No! But imagine if he knew that we knew. What do you think he would do to retain his position, and ... his wife? We have a thing called trackers which the viewers don't realise is attached to the video content. We will therefore know every little perversion they watch.

"So," said Reklem, "he'd not just sell the family silver, but he'd give away the country's gold. Got you."

Gerry smiled, "I see you've been well briefed."

1978. The Sting

The coffee cups were long empty, and the blue sky was dotted with quickly moving fluffy clouds. Reklem was completely sold. Sold on what exactly, she didn't know, but it all seemed to make sense.

Gerry said, "That's not all! After the gold has, let's say, been relocated with the blessing of the minister, he would be faced with another problem. Any ideas?" questioned Gerry with a smile.

"Currencies," he continued, "are linked to gold. Money is its substitute. No gold equals worthless money. Now if people found out that the anchor of the ship, gold, had gone ... well, you can imagine.

At this point we would *encourage* the ministers to print money taking the population's eyes off their missing asset. Thinking about it, their poor judgement put these corruptible individuals there in the first place.

The printing would be diversionary at first, but then it would be inflationary, as people would think that they were getting richer.

Property prices would rise with inflation to use an example. But in reality they're not really rising at all!

The worlds wealth would be a ship, anchorless, with a dragging chain and adrift, at the mercy of the storms that frequent the Seas of Inflation. Riots would ensue at the realisation, and food would be the scarce new currency. Money would be worth nothing. That! Is the moment when we would move in on the markets and buy the West with *their* missing gold."

Gerry recrossed his legs and sat back, smiled, and said, "And we win ... Do *you* like sex, Angela?"

***

The Fourth Handshake

1999. Koh Samui. Who is the Big Man?

Nurse Sawa was alone and realised the crashing waves in front of her were the only means of escape. Little did she know that her problems had just become a lot worse. The Big Man returned to the hotel from O. P. Bungalows holding the fake key.

He looked at his confused bodyguard, who raised his eyebrows and shrugged his shoulders. The menace of the tall Big Man was considerable, even though he was fat and out of shape. He was ruthless and the piercing stare from his steely blue eyes was terrifying to many.

Despite his privileged education, his philosophy, after many years of brutality, was that violence (or its threat) should be the first line of negotiation in every instance - which was understood by anyone that encountered him. Being of high intelligence, he had worked out the current situation and made his way toward the side alley of the hotel.

His bodyguard instinctively followed. The Big Man stopped and returned to the other side of the hotel instead, presuming his other bodyguards had followed the obvious route down the side to the sea.

"Where are you going, Khun Gerry?" said the Thai bodyguard.

Gerry gave him a stare as he hurriedly walked past. The bodyguard asked no further questions and followed as they ran toward the sea. After a short while the path led onto the rocks which shone in the darkness as large breaking waves were illuminated by the hotels lighting.

Sawa ran suddenly and broke cover, heading terrified into the huge breaking waves. The two men on the ground saw her immediately and gave chase. A freezing wave knocked Sawa down as she entered the sea, and she quickly tried to regain her footing before the next breaker. The two men didn't follow and watched from a short distance. Sawa ducked underwater to avoid the next wave, which thundered over her. The storm out in the bay must have been pretty serious to unleash such power.

"Sawa," boomed a voice over the noise of the sea, cutting into Sawa's imaginary plan. She jumped and turned around and looked up to find Gerry and his bodyguard towering above her. This was it, she thought, and stood up from behind her plant cover. Gerry briefly looked at her and turned around to head back to the vehicles.

"Bring her," he instructed. The bodyguard grabbed her by the arm and led her to the road, followed by the other two sheepish men who knew they were in trouble. Sawa presumed she had met the Big Man.

She was pushed into the back of the truck, and Gerry sat next to her. The others got into the vehicles, and Gerry said, "Five Palms."

They sped off into the night, and Sawa was aware she had not been blindfolded. This, in her mind, equalled death. If they were going to let her live, they would have followed the original procedure of blindfolding her, so she started to formulate a plan, which would have to be implemented with immediate effect.

"You're a bad girl, Sawa," said Gerry, breaking the silence in the dark car.

Sawa recognised his voice from the earlier interrogation. So, Gerry *was* the 'Big Man'. Sawa couldn't think what to do and time was fast running out.

"You gave me a fake, wasting my time. No one plays with me like that. You're going to tell me where the original is. Do you have any idea what you're playing with here?" Gerry asked without emotion, in his upper-class English accent. His stare forward didn't waver. The driver tried to see Sawa in his rear-view mirror but couldn't, as she was behind him.

"It's only a key. I was told to cut the extra," she lied.

"You know these keys can't be replicated. They're unique."

"I was given the key, so I don't know," she pleaded, with her normally calm voice wavering.

This break in her voice convinced Gerry that she was lying.

Sawa held onto the door handle tightly. The vehicle slowed to navigate a corner, and she threw the door open and jumped out. The door flew into the air as a passing car hit it, whilst pulling Sawa into the road, still holding on. The unfortunate driver then unwittingly ran over Sawa.

Both vehicles stopped.

Sawa was dead.

Gerry looked down from the truck where the door had once been. "Drive."

***

1999 Koh Samui. Yaba

Detective Gunn decided to pay another visit to see if Nurse Sawa was at home in Bang Rak, except now he had authority to search her premises. He sat outside a while to see if anything stirred - but nothing did. So he got out of the car and went up the stairs. The door was closed this time, meaning someone had been around - it was open on his last visit. Maybe a courteous neighbour obliged, although he doubted that judging by the area's reputation. He called Sawa's name, but all remained quiet, so he turned the handle, and the door opened.

The place seemed to be as it was when he was there previously which didn't feel right to him. This street was known to him for Yaba. A common drug in plentiful supply and a fair amount of it had found its way to the immediate area. If anyone had been around they would have turned the place over looking for money, but this was not the case. Sawa's bed had remained unmade, and the tiny house had an air as if no one had been inside for a period of time.

A cockroach broke cover to scuttle in the shadows to the kitchen area. Gunn followed and found a sink with unwashed dishes wallowing in dirty water. The narrow kitchen had a slatted windows which effectively let in brown sunlight through the dusty glass, making the stale humidity unbearable. There was nothing to find in the kitchen, Gunn surmised, and wandered back around the bed. He looked underneath, then he inspected the wardrobe. Nothing! A photo album was on the chair with the usual suspects inside. Mother, father, sisters...relatives or so he presumed. He decided to keep it and was disturbed by a call on his phone. It was his colleague.

"Hi, Gunn." He answered.

"Gunn, can you do me a favour as you're not very far?"

"Sure, far from what?

His colleague continued (in Thai), "It's a weird one, a tourist rang in last night and described a car accident with a fatality. Here's the thing, he gave the location and the details of what happened. He was obviously shaken and scared. We told him to wait and when we arrived there was nothing. No tourist, no cars, nothing."

"So, you want me to check it out?"

"Yes, but there's more. There's blood on the street. Somebody seems to have attempted to cover this up. And... the tourist is missing."

"OK, I'm on my way." Gunn took the photo album, closed the door, and left.

1998. The Year Before. London – Moscow – Bangkok

The young couple, G and Nastya, got off the underground and found the check in for Aeroflot at Heathrow's Terminal 4. This airline had a fearsome reputation for being awful, but all the other airlines to Thailand were completely booked up, so they had no other option. Christmas in Thailand, they realised, was not an original idea. Tired from the early morning start they joined a long queue for the check in.

An African man's stare caught G's eye, and he approached them and asked the couple for a favour. They had no clue who this person was but asked what the favour was anyway. He asked if they could take a bag for him as he had misjudged the weight of his luggage and that he would be refused onto the plane, unless he left his suitcase behind.

"That's a very good story," said G looking the man straight in the eyes. The man momentarily stood and stared back, and without any comments moved along to someone else in the queue asking the same question. G couldn't quite believe the audacity of the man as the queue shuffled slowly forward.

They boarded the plane and were pretty surprised at its condition after all the stories and rumours about Aeroflot. They imagined getting on a plane out of the 40s that would probably require a push start. Instead, they were greeted by a very pleasant air hostess who spoke perfect English, on this most modern of planes. They found their seats and waited for the take-off which wasn't delayed. They were on the way to Moscow for a connecting flight where they would have to wait a few hours.

"This seems too good to be true," said G, tucking into some delicious in-flight food.

"I know," said Nastya, "but who cares, this is fantastic!"

The plane landed in one piece and on time. They were directed in the dark to a lounge for the connecting flight which would have to navigate the freezing blizzard outside. Their smiles were to be their last for quite some time as from this point on they were about to completely understand that Aeroflot's reputation wasn't mythical at all!

The cunning Russian company had lulled them into a false sense of security. It became clear, in boxers' terms, that they'd been softened up for the uppercut that was to follow in the form of a dark, unlit Moscow waiting room. The monumental, foodless, eight-hour delay was another blow. Surely, they thought things couldn't get any worse, but they were wrong! Aeroflot had other 'one two's', with a kick in the ribs on the canvas to follow later.

They buckled up and prepared for a flight from hell with their predominantly overweight, shaven headed, Russian co-passengers, all having a penchant for Scholl sandals and socks. Nastya's beautiful red bob of hair and G's southern European complexion seemed completely out of place within these ugly, dated surroundings.

The ground crews rapidly de-iced the plane's wings and left.

"They've missed some!" said G helplessly, as they stared out the window. The temperature outside by now had steadied at -33. The plane took off!

Horrendous food was served (including some extraordinary, boiled chicken which they likened to bubble gum). Their virtual boxing match with Aeroflot was followed by a real fight, watched on by passengers who all seemed to be smoking cigarettes. They stood up from their seats which moved as they weren't bolted down properly.

This new development kept the couple awake for the remaining nine-hour journey, hoping the same construction team weren't involved in attaching the jet engines to the plane.

Finally, the Thai jungles below came into vision through the portholes, revealing a misty morning haze and a faintly visible sun, so famed for rising in the East. They had made it, although the remaining half hour of the flight seemed to them to take forever. Bracing themselves for the wheels to fall off the plane landed hazard free. An uncontrolled passenger melee ensued when the doors finally opened, created by the surge to get out.

The passengers expecting the foul, sweaty, smoky air to be replaced by perfumed fresh breezes from outside was about to be challenged. They were about to discover that Bangkok's fresh air rating was probably lower than that of the plane's interior.

Exhausted, and after waiting for the *fat and muscle* stampede to get off the plane, they made their way through customs via endless travellators finally staggering out of the airport straight into a nest of vultures, otherwise known as Bangkok taxi drivers.

Their original plan was thrown out the window as they had missed the pre-booked (long-gone) connecting flight to Koh Samui. A conversation with a fellow western *survivor* who was heading in the same direction was had. Between them, they concocted a mad plan 'b' to get a taxi together, to Krabi, instead of waiting a further four hours for the next flight (unaware that the distance was around 550 km). The price, they equated, would be roughly the same. The wisdom of the plan after 48 hours with no sleep would prove to be fallible.

1998. Taxi to Krabi?

Presented with the plan, a random taxi driver agreed with a disbelieving smile, understanding that Aeroflot had yet again succeeded in *pickling* its passengers' minds. The three unloaded their backpacks into the vehicle after a substantial fare was agreed, even though the driver knew it was nowhere near enough to cover a 550 km drive - but the driver took it anyway and would instigate his standard plan 'A'.

They slumped into the cab, and it hurtled off...straight into Bangkok's famous gridlock. It was an epic jam and in the stifling heat, the car simply came to a stand-still. Gradually edging its way forward meter by meter, the exhausted passengers, close to delirium, peered upwards at the masses of flyovers which gave the impression that they were in some sort of subterranean horror movie - inside an oven!

"They don't show this bit in the adverts," muttered G.

The others thought of a retort, but nothing came to them. They decided it wasn't worth it as they continued on their never-ending journey. Without paying too much attention to where they were, the driver pulled up to a hotel driveway after about two hours. The driver got out and in a strong Thai accent informed his passengers that they were at their destination.

"Here Bangkok," he said. The *survivor*, whose name was Joe stepped forward. Joe insisted in his Chicago accent, "This ain't no ferry port, we said ferry port, Krabi,". The driver gave him a menacing stare, before replying.

A heated but pointless discussion ensued, whilst the taxi driver continued to unload their bags. "This Bangkok," he reiterated. He then got into his cab and drove off with their money. In boxing terms, this was a knockout!

"So, if a taxi from the airport to Bangkok is £300," quipped Joe, "how fuckin' much is it for a McDonalds around here?"

A smile was given by all, but this wasn't their laughing moment as they had been dumped outside the exclusive Shangri-La hotel miles from their intended destination. An unsure doorman helped them load their bags onto a brass trolley and led them into a cool, palatial foyer.

"This I can live with. Let's stay a night, I can't go on," said Nastya, and G agreed.

"Dudes, I can't afford this. I'm going to make my way south, to Samui. You guys look me up if you're around, here's my work number."

They shook hands and Joe's warm smile and green eyes left G and Nastya in no doubt that they should meet again. Joe disappeared with his backpack and the couple were shown to their luxurious room, disbelieving that Joe had decided to carry on after such an ordeal.

The next day they indulged in a silver service treat by the pool, where the waiter came with a trolley with the breakfasts under silver covers. When G and Nastya were seated, he simultaneously revealed the feast underneath.

"You don't get this every day in Slough," mused G, "I can't get over how affordable this is, it's unreal. Can we live here?"

The unexpected hypothetical question sowed a seed and lingered in their minds.

The hotel's gardens and pools were an oasis of peace and tranquillity wedged in amongst the never-ending mayhem that persisted outside.

"Time for some culture, don't you think?" said Nastya lying on her sunbed admiring the luxury.

"And some debauchery after," added G.

"Sure, as you wish."

"So, I suggest a visit to the backpackers Mecca, the Khao San Road, which *is* a must... and then the Golden Temple," enthused G, holding his *Lonely Planet* guidebook.

"Sounds great... and the debauchery?"

"Pat Pong."

"I've heard of that place."

"There's a reason. Let's do it!"

When they came out of the foyer, the dirty, intense humidity hit them like a sledgehammer. They felt like animals caught in headlights as they froze and stared at the mayhem all around.

"What just happened? We go from civilisation, go through a door and end up in the third world. This is incredible. Where's the sky gone?"

They looked up at the thin, smoggy, blue strip of sky that was squeezed in-between architecturally unloved blocks towering forty plus floors above them. The Sukhumvit Skytrain railway station, accessed by substantial concrete staircases, cast a long shadow on the eight lanes of jammed traffic below.

Unplanned shops, of all descriptions, were fronted by a long street market selling unidentifiable foods many resembling intestines. G and Nastya unconvinced that the flies, (warded off by makeshift fans with small cloths attached to their blades) was not the main problem and declined a toothless, beckoning smile from one of the elderly lady vendors.

Sweating profusely, Nastya's request for an immediate shower was interrupted by the hotel porter who noticed the couple's reaction and went to hail them a taxi.

"No, let's stay with this...Tuk-Tuk?" said G.

Nastya stunned by the 'theatre' around her, agreed, and they got into a waiting open air vehicle instead. They joined a posse of other Tuk-Tuks, filled with Falang (foreigners in Thai), weaving their way in and out of stationary heavy polluting cars - most of which were on their way to seek out activities that would probably be illegal in their home countries.

The evening was soon upon them, and they finished a simple fish meal in a restaurant.

"I don't think that should kill us."

"Fingers crossed," replied Nastya.

"Pat Pong," and G smiled.

"Go for it."

They took another Tuk-Tuk and got off when it could go no further at their destination, due to the throng of the densely packed tourists. Here they found 'fakes' of every description. Jewellery, watches, clothes and bags one of which Nastya couldn't resist. They drank at numerous Go-Go bars and drunkenly accepted tickets to a heavily touted event called, 'The flying fuck'.

The giggling, scantily clad salesgirls led the couple into a bar. Here was a crowd, in a similar state to G and Nastya, readying for the main event. The loud music and smoky air added to the seediness of the impending star act.

Finally, a girl with a 'strap on', who sat on a trapeze, was illuminated above. She launched herself, to the delight of the drunken customers, towards a stationary naked bottom some few yards ahead of her. This bottom was part of the anatomy of a girl who was bending over braced for the collision whilst holding onto a chair. The thudding slap of flesh was met with more drunken cheers and applause.

"As if," shouted G into Nastya's ear. The rest of the evening was a blur, and it was fortunate for them that the Shangri La was a well know landmark to the taxi drivers.

They awoke the next morning scarcely believing this *other world* that they had just landed on. A world of luxury, poverty and anything goes. They were totally sold on Thailand and couldn't wait to devour more. They booked tickets to Krabi on the understanding they could always come back to this Bangkok mayhem whenever they wanted to.

***.

Another coincidence

"That's more like it," said G as they glimpsed the sea in between the stunning limestone karst mountains for the first time from the coach window. They had finally made it to Krabi after another long, eight-hour journey from the capital.

"When she leapt off that chair on the trapeze do you really think her, you know, went in?" asked Nastya with a saucy smile.

"Unlikely." said G, looking down his nose at Nastya who was resting on his shoulder.

"Wanna try?"

G really couldn't believe his luck with this new insatiable girl he'd found. She sneakily grabbed his crotch, as they disembarked, and G instinctively pushed her away, hoping that no one else saw. Nastya grinned at his coyness as she lifted her backpack over her shoulder.

G decided to draw a line in the sand and retaliate by squeezing Nastya's breast. Nastya being Nastya, didn't push him away despite a few glances from other Thai passengers,

"So, you wanna do this now big man?" joked Nastya.

G shook his head and backed off to the relief of the others.

They had intense passionate sex that night, a waterfall of energy and emotion. It cleared the *decks* from their travelling ordeal. However, unbeknown to them, they were about to embark on a journey from which they would not survive. They would never see Bangkok again.

***

The next day, they sat at a reggae café overlooking the mesmeric sea which gently caressed the shores pure white sands. G leant back on an old sun-bleached wooden chair and momentarily lost control making him fall backwards, hitting the table to his rear.

"I'm so sorry," said G to the person sitting behind, sitting up quickly realising he'd spilt the man's coffee.

"Not to worry, no issues," said Gerry.

Gerry stood up and wiped the coffee residue off his trunks and

Nastya leapt out of her chair to help.

"No problem, seriously no problem," said Gerry insistently.

"So sorry, I'm Nastya and this is G my boyfriend, he's not very good with chairs," and they both looked down at her hapless lover. "Again, no problem," said Gerry and offered his hand to pull up G.

"You guys on holiday?"

"Yes we are, and what a place. Do you live here? You look like you do."

"Sort of, I live on Koh Samui."

"Oh! We met a guy called Joe on the flight over, he's going to Koh Samui too. I think he lives there as well... he's from Michigan - don't suppose you know him?"

"There's quite a few people on the island, but... I may," said the tanned young Gerry trying not to be sarcastic.

"Smart question," interjected Nastya, *with* sarcasm looking at G. She continued, "How long you here for Gerry? - and are we in the best place? These Lonely Planet and Rough Guides I feel, are written by people of dubious tastes. All the backpackers here are taking the advice of people who they know nothing about. Psycho killer stamp collector's advice on where to go in Thailand – that sort of thing."

Gerry laughed, "Stamps are hard to find here, but no, you're not doing badly here. I'm staying for a week in the bungalows over there. Where are you staying?"

"Same, seems to be about the best spot... and our time here is... not sure. How do you better perfection?"

"Indeed," said Gerry in his plummy English accent. He continued, staring at G's watch, "I see you've been shopping in Pat Pong along the way,"

"We *have* - how on earth do you know that? G asked.

"Well judging by your watch, I know of no other places that make Rolox's."

Confused, G looked down and noticed that his watch was absolutely - a *Rolox,* and not the intended Rolex. He turned his wrist to Nastya, showing the watch face, and they burst out laughing at the spelling error. This interaction cemented G and Nastya's first holiday friend, and they spent the day together laughing, swimming and eating.

They met in the evening and watched the renowned beach fire dancers do their dangerous routines, occasionally burning the odd onlooker (with spits of fire from the burning ropes used in the act). One girl was particularly eye catching to all, and very good. She was blonde and had large breasts, which were the star act to many of the watching males.

"I know her," said Gerry looking at G, who pretended to be amazed by the fire act and not the girl. "*She's* a living fire," he shouted above the loud music. "In the right job, German...lives here. We used to date and the way we met was quite unique."

"How so," said G, fixated by the girl, which hadn't gone unnoticed by Nastya.

"We sat at a bar, at opposite ends and I was watching her give out a piece of paper to all the guys that came up to her. She was alone so moths to a flame, you know?"

The music got louder.

"The guys read the paper, smiled, and left... without fail."

"What was the paper about?" asked G, now beginning to show interest.

"Exactly my thoughts," replied Gerry, "so I wandered around to her and asked what was written on the paper, *before*... she gave it to me. Turned out it was every conceivable answer to a pickup question.

My name is Tina.

I'm from Germany.

I live here.

No! I haven't been to Phi Phi.

I'm 25.

I've been here for a month.

I don't have a boyfriend.

...and so on. It was brilliant. I mean how do you follow that?"

"How *did* you follow that?"

"I asked her if she wanted a shag."

G's attention was now fully focused on Gerry. "You didn't? And did she?"

"She did. I think she was so bored she gave up" and at that moment, Tina coincidentally turned and gave Gerry a smile in the middle of her routine.

The show lasted for a short while after.

1998. The Invitation

Gerry woke with a heavy head resulting from the drinking that continued long after the fire dancers had stopped. Tina had joined them but didn't stay. Tina confused Gerry by blowing hot and cold towards any idea of a relationship. Gerry would have liked this but figured it didn't look like it was on the cards - he considered her to be out of his league, in the wrong direction. As magnificent and rich as he thought he was, he realized that she clearly preferred fit young men with free spirits...which he was not. Money couldn't buy her beauty, and he reluctantly accepted he was no god in the shape department.

Gerry was packing in response to a mail to return to Koh Samui. He was interrupted by a knock on the door.

"Hi G, come on in."

"How you feeling?" asked G.

"Not great," smiled Gerry.

"Packing? I thought you were here for a week?"

"So did I," said Gerry, "but I've been called back to my house in Samui."

"You have a *house* in Samui? Wow." said G. Is it on the beach?"

"It's close, but in the jungle." Gerry continued and lied, "It was an inheritance. It's nice, I have to say. Tell you what - why don't you both come and stay if you've got time?"

At that moment Nastya poked her head around the door.

"Perfect timing," said G, "we've just been invited to Gerry's own house in Samui. Whaddya think?"

"Well, that's the second invitation there in a week. Sounds like a plan. Thank you, Gerry," said Nastya hesitantly.

"Great, when?" asked G.

"Your shout," said Gerry, "in your own time."

"Are you working there?" asked Nastya.

"A bit, I'm actually a junior minister for the conservatives in the UK, and as I have connections here, they give me Far East assignments."

"Bloody hell, do you need staff?" quipped G.

"You could be my drinks taster. You seem pretty clued up and talented in that department, judging by last night."

They laughed and after a brief discussion agreed to meet in a weeks' time.

G and Nastya left and walked amongst beautiful flora along a sandy path which cut through gorgeous tropical jungle. This led to the sea from the bungalows, which were set immediately below the dramatic vertical karst cliffs.

"I don't like him," said Nastya out of the blue on their stroll.

"What!"

"Something about him, not sure what."

"Don't you want to go? I bet he's got a stunning house...and it's free," pleaded G.

They arrived at the beach café and ordered coffees.

"So, you don't want to go?" reiterated G in a non-confrontational manner.

"No, we'll go, but I'm not sure of him... that's all."

They sat in a moments silence and proceeded to have the English way of settling an issue, by both stating their opposite position only to finally settle on the side of least resistance.

"So, let's go," said Nastya, and squeezed G's hand with a smile. G really wanted to go so he agreed.

They had some food at the bar and G couldn't let go of Nastya's resistance to a free luxury stay in Koh Samui. It made no sense to him.

"What don't you like about him? He's done nothing controversial."

"Let it go, I have my reasons."

"What are they? Come on, I'm intrigued"

"There's something you don't know about me."

"I'm sure there's lots I don't know about you, so what's this particular mystery?"

"Okay, you wanna hear it?

"Yes, I 'wanna' hear it so what is it?"

"I can see auras."

A silence followed.

"What? What are you talking about?"

"I see things, things that most people can't see, and I can see if someone is good or bad."

"You can see if someone is good or bad," said G a little sarcastically.

"I find I'm receptive to energy - the supernatural, call it what you will," said Nastya.

"No kidding?"

"Sometimes," she continued, "I see people walking amongst other people, who are not there, and the other people can't see them. But I can! I've learnt to control this a little bit".

"Really? I never knew this," said G, now captivated.

"Gerry has a bad aura, literally. There's a dark shadow around him. Silver auras are receptive, and the scale goes down to dark. Gerry is dark. I feel uncomfortable with our new acquaintance."

"Ooookaay," said G now revaluating the situation. "I tell you what, why not find Joe Dude and tell Gerry we'll catch up with him at his house later?"

"Really? That would make me feel better. OK," said an obviously relieved Nastya. "Thank you."

"Of course. We're a team." G paused a moment, "Can you see anyone now?"

"What?"

"Spirits, you know, people wandering around?" said G in a slightly mocking tone.

"Well... yes, I can," replied Nastya.

It took a moment for G to digest this, "What?"

"The man over there has a companion he can't see. He's standing over him. He's very old."

G saw nothing except the man having a coffee. G got up, walked over, hovered by the man, saw nothing, and looked back at Nastya shrugging his shoulders.

"Can I help you?" said the man turning around in his chair.

"Sorry, no, but my girlfriend said there's a man standing over you, a ghost." They both turned and looked at Nastya.

"Excuse me?" said the man.

The *ghost* beckoned Nastya to join them, to which Nastya obliged and came over.

"Hi, I'm Nastya." And you sir are ...?"

"Grandfather George," replied the apparition - unheard by the others. Nastya repeated his answer out loud.

The man sat up, completely confused upon receiving the unexpected information that *Grandfather George* was about. "Who are you?" he asked Nastya.

The ghost continued unheard, *"I've been trying to reach him for years but nothing I can do makes him aware of my presence. I see you can help."*

"He won't believe me George; can you tell me something personal about your relationship?"

The others continued to stare at Nastya talking to fresh air.

"Tell him his mother sold the train set on top of the wardrobe, and that I loved to play piano but had to sell it to make space in the living room," George continued.

Nastya relayed this information to the man who started to look all around in disbelief. "How did you know that? Do I know you?"

G looked on aghast. He had nothing to say. George asked Nastya to let the man know he wasn't sad and was always watching over him, before disappearing into the distance. Nastya passed this information on and informed the man that George had gone.

"Thank you," said the man. "I, I don't know what to say?"

"Nothing to say," replied Nastya. "We have to go now. G?" and she gestured to leave.

"Sure, er nice meeting you," and G shook the man's hand and caught up with Nastya. The man sat down completely confused and watched them leave.

"That was incredible, I never knew."

"Well, you do now," and Nastya gave G a glowing smile.

1998. Phuket to Khao Sok to Samui

They left Krabi a little earlier due to their new arrangements. With Gerry's house no longer being an option, they contacted Joe via an internet café (the new revolution in communication for travellers). Joe was thrilled that they were coming and advised them to stay at a cheap place he knew, on Chaweng Beach by the lake, called Charlie's Huts - 100 baht a night.

Before they went to Khao Sok they stopped off before the link road to the mainland, at a beach called Surin. Unlike the other beaches of Phuket, Surin had no road running along it, so the beach bars had direct access to the sea. The connecting coach left daily from the car park, so they decided to stay a night or two and sample some of the reggae bars. This innocuous unplanned stop was going to prove to be quite a significant piece in the jigsaw of what remained of their life.

They went to the daily street market in the car park selling poor quality fakes, when G looked down a connecting road. The light began to turn hazy and then through the fog G thought he saw his doppelganger - except he looked a lot older. He stared a moment, then his doppelganger started to look his way. Embarrassed at staring, G looked away. The haze began to clear and sharpen, and G realised that his doppelganger had gone. G looked around and turned to look behind him, but the apparition was nowhere to be seen, just people milling around wares arranged on tables. He thought no more of it.

They decided not to spend more time at Surin and instead take a slight diversion on the way to Koh Samui to stay at an inland mountain lake called Khao Sok. What appealed to them most about this place was the floating accommodation – wooden huts on rafts connected by floating bamboo walkways.

Their stay was largely uneventful, apart from being scared to death by unidentified animals running around on the roof at night. They found the place magical but off season as all the rivers had dried up and few tourists were around. The most memorable thing they did was to get drunk and count ants on a wall using a magnifying glass.

Upon leaving Khao Sok, they excitedly embarked on another freezing coach to Samui, which took about 12 hours including the ferry crossing. The Thais, as they were learning, didn't do things in half measures, so therefore maximum cranked-up air-con was what they now understood to be the (luxury) norm.

Shivering and partially deaf from the Thai 'comedy' TV programme set at full volume (this combination made the vehicle super-VIP in the ticket sellers' eyes). The Thai humour was lost on them - meringue pies lobbed at unsuspecting faces, over-theatrical "boinging" noise effects and raucous laughter, didn't cut the mustard. They equated the experience, to a grounded version of their Aeroflot journey – zero.

The last part of the journey was via a *Song Thaew* bus which was an experience in itself. They found it great fun and G hung on the back standing on the bumper with another tourist, whilst Nastya and a few other passengers sat in the glassless passenger compartment. They arrived at the very shabby, pot- holed, mud street that was Chaweng High Street.

It was basic and lined with a few bars and some two-storey buildings - one notably having a ladyboy bar on its roof. After resisting the less than tempting invitations to join them from the towering ladyboys with Adam's apples and heels, they quickened their pace. Hurriedly escaping the teasing ladyboys they finally arrived at a bridge which they had been told to cross by Joe.

Here lay The Green Mango, a Chaweng institution (it's now been relocated to the beach). They followed Joe's directions and found the unmissable Reggae Pub on the lake. They approached the two-storey wooden shack, with 'Johnny be Good' by Peter Tosh blaring out. Joe was waiting.

1998. The Reggae Pub – Charlie's Huts

"Duuuuuuude," said G and they gave each other a big warm hug. Nastya followed suit. They sat down outside and watched the bar fill up with twenty-something hippy revellers who, judging by their smiles, were having the times of their lives in this *anything goes* country. The three stayed until they were a little drunk and Joe suggested they find their bungalow accommodation.

They walked across the lake on a narrow wooden walkway which snaked its way through tall reeds which grew densely all around. After about ten minutes, they were there on the moonlit white sands of Chaweng Beach and the famous 'A' framed bungalows of Charlie's Huts. The silence was broken by the muffled roar of white waves breaking on the distant reef.

"This really *is* paradise," said G to Nastya, "and *you* live here dude," G continued mock shaking his head, looking at Joe.

"Sure do. Guys I'll leave you to it and see you in the morning, I have early stuff to do. I'm just down the road - have fun and catch up for breakfast." They high fived, and he left. Their hut was cheaply made of varnished wicker panels which gave it a toffee colour. It was the simplest construction possible, comprising of two panels propped up against each other in an 'A' shape on a raised wooden floor where lay a mattress with a dubious history. A shower room was within, which was basically a suspended hose.

"I see Joe rates romance above luxury," said G which made Nastya laugh.

They settled in and sat a while looking at the sea drinking a bottle of Sang Tip (another cheap Thai whiskey) before calling it a day.

They awoke early the next morning, with a hangover in crushing heat where the bungalow panels acted like giant radiators powered by the sun. Sand was everywhere inside, and G leapt out of the bed upon discovering a spider's nest above his head.

They got themselves together and ran into the shallow clear sea before heading off to Joe's accommodation. The sky was clear, with the Eagles "Take it Easy'" playing from Joe's house when they arrived. Joe smiled when he saw them approach and they sat on uncomfortable, glazed semi-circular concrete benches arranged around a similar structured circular table, decorated in green and blue mosaic.

The couple told Joe about Gerry and that perhaps they should all meet. Joe explained that his job was selling water coolers and ice machines, and that he had to return unexpectedly to Bangkok, so it was unlikely he could join them. He said he'd be back in a week or so and perhaps meet him then.

"I was expecting you guys later," said Joe to the disappointed couple.

They decided to walk to the beach and sit by the sea at a café where a small rocky island could be seen close to the shore. This marked the end of the reef that was being pounded by waves on its lea side. The wide stretch of sea that lay between the reef and shore was shallow, calm and totally clear.

What G didn't realise was that Nastya knew exactly what geography to expect at this point of the beach even though she'd never been.

***

1998. The future

Nastya left Joe and G and walked along the edge of the sea for about five minutes.

"What's she looking at?" G asked Joe.

"No clue man. She lost something?"

G was puzzled by the intensity at which Nastya was surveying the land behind the beach. It was as if she'd seen something unexpected.

"S'cuse me a mo," and G made his way to Nastya. She saw him in the distance as he made his way towards her, ankle deep in the warm water.

G felt so happy that he occasionally kicked water into the air on his way, "What you lookin' at?" G said, grabbing Nastya around her little waist.

"Something you won't understand."

"What, more ghosts?" and G mock strained his eyes looking landwards.

"No, I'll show you shortly when we get back to the café."

"OK," said G with an air of foreboding, "good or bad?"

"Inexplicable and confusing," replied Nastya, giving G a sideways glance with a short smile. "Come."

Joe watched them turn around, hand in hand and walk back across the hot sunny beach. "You guys found somethin'?" he shouted.

"She won't tell me," joked G, and they sat down.

"You ready for this?" said Nastya, getting her beach bag from under the table.

"Sure," said G, with Joe looking on a little confused.

Nastya reached into the bag and pulled out another small plastic bag - her anxiety in doing so seemed to be on a par with the boys.

She pulled out a postcard and put it on the table. It was the same one Lisa discovered on that snowy day, which had led them to the travel agents. She too still couldn't believe what she was seeing. It was the future, Chaweng's beach future on a postcard.

G and Joe took quite a while to respond. "What on earth is this?", said G holding the card. "Is that here? It can't be? None of this exists."

"Do you recognise this, Joe?" asked Nastya. "Is there a similar beach around here somewhere?"

"Nope, this is here alright. Where'd you get this?" said Joe glancing around at the land. "It's all built up. Check out the chicks in the next-to-nothing knickers," Joe continued, pointing at the G string bikinis.

"Very nice," said G marginally distracted. The age of the card added to the confusion, as it looked about 20 years old.

"OK, let's start," said G. "How long have you had this?

"About a year."

"Did youuuu come to Chaweng with this in mind - er, was this your plan all along. Hey, why didn't you tell me?"

"I didn't think you'd understand."

"Any other nuggets you got in that there bag, girl?" said G in a mock American southern accent, "Anythang eylse there, I should know abaat?" and G feigned a Clint Eastwood spit.

Laughing, Nastya confirmed the negative.

"So, Lisa knows about this too. Hmm is she here as well? Hiding behind that tree...with all her mates... who she told?"

"No, no, no," said Nastya grabbing G's hand. "I'm as confused as you are."

Nastya batted off a dozen or so other questions with no answers, as they continued to sit staring at the card.

"Is this a sign of something? If anyone would know you would."

"Whaddya mean?" interjected Joe.

"Nastya can see ghosts, the future, auras and stuff," said G, with Nastya frowning at the answer.

"Right," said Joe, nodding sceptically.

"No, I can't fathom this at all," she replied in a steady voice, "but…"

"But what?" repeated G knowing something big was to follow.

"The handwriting on the other side…"

G flipped the card over and read, "Five Trees House, Bohput."

"Yes, I know," said Nastya impatiently, "I'm trying to tell you something," she paused and said, "It's my handwriting."

The expected pause happened, which was finally broken by G saying "What?" looking very carefully again at the card.

G's initial answer to Joe's question regarding the spirits was still filtering down, and this new information blew his mind.

The warm sea breeze rustled the café's dry palm leaf roof, and the sun's heat was at its peak as the group tried to work some sense into the situation.

"Let's walk," announced G, "and check this out," as he pointed to where the buildings should be. They agreed, stood up together and proceeded to leave.

"Hey guys, probably not a bad idea to pay," said a young man sitting on the shaded next table, who had overheard much of the group's conversation.

"Excuse me? Oh yes, good idea," said G, "Mr…?" and he fumbled in his pockets as the waiter appeared.

"Gunn," replied the man. "Youuuu, like snowy Chelsea pubs."

G lifted his head, confused and stared at Gunn, trying to digest what he'd just said.

"C'mon!" said Nastya.

"Coming," said G.

"G," and he gave his hand to Gunn to shake. Gunn shook it.

"Have we met?" and before Gunn could answer Joe shouted over.

"Er, gotta go," and G turned away and ran towards the others.

1998. No blood!

Detective Gunn watched the group wander off down Chaweng beach and didn't fully understand what he'd just overheard. He couldn't believe the coincidence of recognising the couple from the snowy Chelsea pub from all those years ago when he was a London student. The girl's distinctive red bob hairstyle had rung the bells.

Gunn was unaware that this by chance meeting would be a vital piece of a murder jigsaw. Ironically it would be for a future murder that hadn't taken place yet.

For now, he was trying to straighten out his mind at Chaweng beach. He was trying to focus on his first murder assignment, which was confusing and needed answers.

He was probably offered the case as nobody else in the police department could fathom it out. Lots of blood and no bodies were the basics of the crime and no one had reported anyone missing. The blood in the case had been found by a farmer in a banana plantation accessed by a small dirt road. Tests had been done on the blood, which was splattered everywhere, and it was established that there were two different types.

What made it a murder investigation was the sheer *amount* of blood. The unlucky two would have had very little blood left in their veins after the loss. The remaining amount could not sustain life so therefore there had to be bodies, making the plantation a murder site. Gunn had searched the immediate area with his chosen team but found nothing. No blood trails leading to bodies, nothing!

He found out who farmed the land and who it belonged to, which turned out to be a local mafia man going by the name of P. Bun Ma.

P. Bun Ma was to be the next stop for Gunn after he finished his papaya salad, which he found very 'espicy' (Thai/English for off-the-scale heat). P. Bun Ma was only a five-minute drive down the road at Cheong Mon beach, which Gunn proceeded to visit in the searing afternoon heat. He was told that P. Bun Ma ran a travel agency, which Gunn presumed to be a front of some kind as P. Bun Ma was very, very wealthy.

His known wealth came from land inheritance, which was primarily expensive beachfront. In the past poor farmers (which was P. Bun Ma) were given this, as waterfront was considered worthless and potentially dangerous. As a result, many of the lowly farmers, by default, became the new *elite* with a downside. Disputes were settled in the old-fashioned way giving rise to mafias. Gunn was therefore not looking forward to the meeting, as he knew the police were probably in P. Bun Ma's pocket.

He came off the dirt road which led away from the sea and saw the wooden house he was looking for. The glass front had stickers advertising wild adventures for tourists, including elephant rides and tickets for boats to the Full Moon Party. Taking off his shoes he went into the office and was greeted by an older white man called Terry.

"Can I help you," said Terry in an Australian accent.

"Yes, I'm trying to find P. Bun Ma, is he here?"

"Who's asking?" said Terry in a very friendly manner.

"Detective Gunn."

"Oh right, er, just one moment, er do I know you?" said Terry.

"I don't think so."

"No, sorry, you just looked familiar," and Terry disappeared around the back not wishing to know what the visit was about.

"Please go through," said Terry upon returning and gestured towards the back office.

"Thank you," and Gunn passed through, bending his head slightly as the door was designed for smaller native Thais.

1998. Meeting Martin.

The group wandered up Chaweng beach with Nastya leading the way, holding the card.

"Who was the guy at the café?" asked Nastya.

"Not sure, I think he knew us."

"Really? Didn't recognise him. Did you?"

"No. He said his name was Gunn," Replied G. "Do you know him, Joe?"

"Don't know, wasn't really looking."

The subject was dropped as they had reached their destination according to the card's photograph. There was no hotel, only dunes and grass. They came off the beach and onto the land which was flat and had a beach road running along it - inland. The wind blew making the humidity bearable in the direct sunlight. There were two well-dressed men standing in front of them, who were clearly not tourists and seemed interested in the plot, so Nastya, as bold as ever, marched up to the Westerners.

"Hi guys, my name's Nastya."

They both turned around and stared at her, obviously captivated by her good looks. They looked behind her and saw G and Joe.

"Hi, I'm Martin," said one of the men, "Kunsmann. Can we help?"

"Yes, maybe, do you recognise this?" and she showed them the card.

Their eyes widened as they recognised the picture.

"Where on earth did you get this? We are looking to build this...here!"

"I found it in England in a café," replied Nastya. By then G and Joe had joined them and they all shook hands.

"This is an artist's impression we had made up, but this looks like an actual photograph of the real thing. The people look ...so real." said Martin.

He turned the card over and after reading what was on the back, Martin looked at his colleague with a wry smile.

"This is confidential information you know." said the other man.

"Are you the owners?" asked G.

"No," said the man, "Khun Gerry Absalom is. And Five Palms House on the card... is where he lives. Where did you get this again?" he asked.

"Gerry?" said G and Nastya simultaneously.

"You know him?" asked Martin.

"Yes! This is all too weird," said G, after explaining the situation. "The guy Gunn in the café. Chance meeting you Martin...who also knows Gerry, and... all instigated by a card found ages ago in a café. Beer is needed."

"Sorry. We have to go now" said Martin, so we'll have to pass. Here's my number." and Martin gave them his card.

"Director of the Amari Group." said G, nodding his head impressed.

"I guess we'll have to see Gerry now," said G to Nastya sitting in front of their bungalow. "Fate is beating a path to his door, which apparently is Five Palms House."

"I guess." repeated Nastya knowing it wasn't right.

Picking up on Nastya's unease, G gave her a squeeze. They decided it was meant to be and G assured Nastya that it would be fine and probably fun. Nastya smiled but remained unconvinced as every fibre in her body warned her against the visit.

G now realised that he had come across Gunn before but wasn't sure when or where.

$$***.$$

They decided that as much as they loved beaches, they'd prefer not to have most of it in their bed, so an accommodation 'upgrade' was discussed. During a lunch in a local beach café, they found a brochure advertising an idyllic bungalow set in the jungle on the beach. It was part of a small complex of similar bungalows except this one was directly on the beach. G rang the number, and the landlady confirmed its vacancy, and a meeting was arranged.

It was at Plai Laem beach and when the tuk-tuk took them down the unmade road they couldn't believe the paradise that lay in front of them. They saw the bungalow at the end of a terrace of five similar properties, surrounded by vegetation and the dominant banana palms.

"You couldn't make this up," said G.

Nastya remained speechless. Across a short strait lay the small uninhabited island of Koh Som. A few palms towered over them and swayed in the sea breeze which was the only sound that could be heard. In the vivid daylight, the Bay of Bohput could also be seen in the distance. The tuk-tuk left and they stood at the base of the short staircase that led to the wraparound terrace and building. After the landlady O showed them around and gave them the key, they sat on the chairs and marvelled at what they had discovered. It was a while before either of them spoke. Lisa finally pulled out a book from her bag.

"What you reading?" asked G.

"It's a funny book about a couple travelling around Thailand, Thailand Diaries, ... oops!" and a photo fell to the floor.

"What's that?"

"An old black and white photo. Must be Lisa's. It's her book."

1998 Dead end

P. Bun Ma was sat behind a chaotic desktop adorned by piles of paperwork and office artifacts. Gunn thought him to be in his fifties and not in the best shape. P. Bun Ma pointed Gunn to sit in the chair in front of him. *Unpredictable power is a scary thing in a human*, Gunn mused as he waited. P. Bun Ma looked up and in his native tongue asked what he could do for him.

It was a strange situation for Gunn as he realised P. Bun Ma was indirectly his boss as he probably knew the police rather well. He decided to tread very carefully.

"I think there's been a double murder on land that you own near a house called Five Palms."

P. Bun Ma sat in silence for a moment and then replied. "I heard." He sat silent again and then said, "No bodies I hear."

Gunn, realising P. Bun Ma was up to speed on the matter confirmed the problem.

"I was wondering if you had any ideas?" Gunn said calmly.

"None." was the reply.

Gunn nodded his head and realised this was pointless if P. Bun Ma had something to hide. Gunn looked around and at the ceiling and stood up.

"Sorry to bother you, I have to do these questions you understand?"

"I do."

Gunn wai'd P. Bun Ma, showing respect and got up to leave.

"I have some ideas," said P. Bun Ma suddenly, "I'll be in touch."

"Oh! OK. Thank you." and Gunn left the room.

Terry was there. "Everything OK?"

"Yes, fine thank you." and they smiled at each other.

Gunn blinked outside when the sunlight hit his eyes, and he walked back in the searing heat to his car.

1998. Nastya's worst nightmare!

Joe had to go and said he'd be back in a week or two as his boss in Bangkok needed him. This made the couple sad as they'd grown fond of his calm and happy persona.

"Shall we see Gerry?" said G over lunch one day. "Our time is running short and I'm more than curious about what is going on. I bet he can put it all into perspective."

"You're right I suppose. Go on, call him." said Nastya unconvinced.

"Just a quick visit, we don't have to stay long... we'll play it by ear."

Nastya nodded again, not showing her fear. But she too felt as if questions needed answering.

They went later to Chaweng high street and found a phone box to make the call. G dialled the number Gerry had given them in Krabi. G smiled reassuringly at the serious Nastya as he did so. "No answer!" said G stating the obvious.

He put the phone down and they stood a moment. Nastya wondered if this was an omen.

They decided to 'take five' and walked to a backpacker restaurant just off the dusty road and ordered papaya salad and chicken fried rice. "No MSG." instructed G to the bored Thai waiter. "Oh! and nit noi (small in Thai) salt." The waiter once again tried to leave as G shouted, "also no sugar!" The waiter by now had broken into a slight trot to get away into the kitchen.

Not sure if the waiter heard or not, G said to Nastya, "They always seem to be in a hurry...to get the wrong order. Why? Am I a deer with no eyes?"

Nastya nodded and then realised what G said, "Sorry what?"

"No I - dea," and G gave Nastya a sideways grin.

Nastya burst out laughing. "You fool. You know me so well already."

"Well, it's nice to make you smile," smirked G. "Shall we check out Gerry's house anyway. He's probably back on Krabi, or London, - in his helicopter. Who knows?"

Nastya sighed and said, "All right then. And then we leave right?"

"Right."

It was the afternoon, so G suggested they take a peek after lunch as it was only a short tuk- tuk ride away from where they were staying. Nastya agreed.

"I have to let Lisa know what we're up to first. Can I send a quick letter? She will wonder."

"Sure," said G.

They found a post office and she gave the postcard with the message to the Thai man behind the counter.

' Hi Honey',

Met a man called Gerry who we're going to visit. I'm really not sure about him, but G likes him. He's an English MP. oooo. Get this. He lives at Five Palms.??? Met him in Krabi. Guy called Martin Kunsmann was at postcard spot. Hotel not built yet? He's with Amari. Coincidence.??? Owned by Gerry!!!!! Talk later hope you're ok. Nastya- G.

Oh met guy called Joe. American. sells water coolers. XXXX' I'll call.

Once the hurried note was dispatched, Nastya looked at G and said, "OK. I'm all yours."

1998. Five Palms

The couple hailed a tuk-tuk to take them fifteen minutes down the coast road towards Bohput and Bang Rak.

They showed the driver a sketch of the 'T' junction near Big Buddha. Five Palms was off a dirt road called Soi Plai Laem 8, which they'd worked out from a local's map. The driver smiled at them when they gave the directions, which didn't fill them with confidence as they now knew the Thais smiled when confused or not fully understanding. The driver took off, swerving to avoid the many potholes that adorned their hot, sweaty journey in the dust. He finally turned off the main road and proceeded up a very steep road. He stopped.

"You go now." said the driver in a strong local accent.

"No. You go further," said G.

"Cannot."

"No, you go more," insisted G, on the deserted banana palmed road.

"Bike on tuk-tuk no good engine. Cannot."

"Oh, I see." Said G and they got out.

"How much?" G asked.

"50 Baht."

The driver turned around and left. Still not sure where they were or indeed if they were on the right road, they continued up the steep incline. Soon after, the road opened up and the trees thinned out. They could see in the near distance an impressive walled structure.

"That's it!" said G. "Five Palms," and he counted out loud the five palm trees that fronted the house.

Nastya took in a deep breath.

"Shall we see if Gerry's home?" asked G rhetorically.

Nastya nodded and they came out of the banana plantation into the open area that lay in front of the house.

"The doors open!" said G enthusiastically.

A Thai man in a smart white Thai jacket and trousers appeared at the entrance.

The couple approached and asked if Gerry was at home. They explained how they knew him, and their detailed knowledge convinced the man to let them in.

He pointed to some luxurious wooden benches on the terrace outside the main house.

"You sit there. Oh! Can you give this to Khun Gerry?" I have to go outside for a moment. He gave them a key.

"Sure," said G.

They walked across a wooden bridge spanning a large pond and sat down.

"This is no good", said Nastya.

G interrupted, "Shh, I can hear him." They heard Gerry talking on the phone through a door which was slightly ajar.

"I know Reklem," said Gerry on the phone in an agitated voice. "Yes...Yes. The Director Kunsmann told me about the meeting, the couple and a guy called Joe. Yes...No.

They *are* dead. I know ...I'll get rid of them later. They're in the secret room... behind the library." Gerry stopped talking and listened momentarily.

"P. Bun Ma told me about a Detective Gunn asking questions...yes, I know, but it's his job. He knows nothing... P. Bun Ma's dealing with that side of things. Trust me, I've got this covered. The couple know nothing. Ok, Ok. Yes... Talk tomorrow." Gerry put the phone down and there was silence in the room.

Gerry came out onto the terrace and to his surprise he saw G and Nastya sitting down. Judging from the looks on their faces, all was not well.

Gerry shook his head sighed and said, "Guys, I'm sorry, but you leave me no option."

Atai watched the events unfold in the distance.

***

Nastya opened her eyes in the darkness and could see some light coming through a crack under a door. She was on the floor in a small damp room in horrendous pain and covered in blood. She saw two bodies next to her and thought she saw G crawling slowly up the stairs back towards the door.

She began to have a very strange experience – she was looking at herself, and then realised she was floating and could look down at G on the stairs - who was in a terrible state. Then she saw the closed cellar door from the hall side and drifted down the hall towards men shouting. She was not visible as she hovered above the men who started to become violent. Then darkness gradually absorbed Nastya's being in the cellar - and she lived no more.

The Fifth Handshake

1999 "Nastya. Is that you?"

Lisa was now sitting upstairs in yet another new home, rented under a false name in Clapham, South London. She had access to money thanks to Timmingham and she was therefore effectively on the government payroll as an undercover agent, which not even Whitehall knew about.

The house was on the north side of Clapham Common on Taybridge Road, in one of the many terraced Victorian houses. The house was of an unusual design internally, as the first-floor rooms were vertically combined with the rear ground floor receptions, giving way to 13-metre-high ceilings with a gallery above. The Common could be seen a few metres down the road from the upstairs front bay window.

Lisa was startled by a knock on the door. As no one except her mother Anna, currently in Corfu, knew where she was. She presumed it could only be Timmingham, meaning it had to be an emergency. She looked out the upstairs bay window and saw that it was not. It was a delivery man. She decided to let him go away and leave a note, as they do - except she heard the front door open.

Lisa stopped momentarily on the upstairs landing on her way down as she heard a girl speak to the delivery man, who in return spoke and wished the girl a good day, before leaving. The girl quietly said thank you, and it was silent once more. Lisa could hear no more sounds and never heard the door close. She stood for a moment trying to work out the situation. She poked her head around the landing to see the front door downstairs. All was quiet and there was no girl to be seen. The door was closed!

"Nastya is that you?" asked Lisa hesitantly. She could have sworn she recognised her friend's voice.

She folded her arms and gingerly went downstairs, looking back towards the rear of the house, when she noticed a piece of paper on the floor by the door. It hadn't been there before!

She stepped over it, and opened the door to see if anyone was there, but there was no one, which she thought odd as she could see a fair way down the road in either direction. She quickly crossed the road for an alternative view, but again, saw no one. She went back to the house and looked down at the paper, bent down, and picked it up. It was from Nastya.

She read the postcard and saw the name Gerry halfway down immediately. She couldn't believe the coincidence. Five Palms House? Surely it couldn't be the same Gerry Absalom. If it was Lisa surmised, she had better warn her, and quickly - not to cross his path.

She guessed Nastya still to be in Koh Samui and decided after a lot of deliberation that she needed to go there as the note had to be a sign. She couldn't phone Nastya as she had no clue as to her exact whereabouts or contact details, plus Lisa was trying to distance herself from everyone she liked, as she could get them into trouble - meaning no information from that quarter.

146

She presumed everyone to consider her a useless friend at this thought. This was the problem in Lisa's mind, how on earth did Nastya know her new address? Then she turned Nastya's letter over - there was no address!

1999. Again!

Everything was hazy. Everything seemed to be floating, unfixed, in a world where gravity had lost. It was very bright, and the sea was blurry which seemed to merge in with the white sand. People walked in slow motion and all sound was muffled.

Gunn was looking seawards and turned around, only to find himself walking downstairs in a very dark environment. Suddenly somehow it was night. He could feel a massive negative force where he was headed but was powerless to stop, even though he wanted to. He felt that the force ahead would absorb him like blotting paper on ink. He shouted, "Come on, come ON, I'm not afraid of you!".

He used what little power was left in his drained arms to take a swing at whatever it was. It was hopeless and he was helpless; he was going to lose. This was it...

Gunn woke up screaming. A man's scream, deep and harrowing. He sat up and looked around and could only see the overhead ceiling fan rotating in silence. Otherwise, all was still. There was a slight breeze outside and the breaking waves could be heard. He lay down again, scared to fall asleep as he didn't want to re-enter the dream. This dream had taken root - this was the third time.

1999 Koh Samui. Terry

Lisa disembarked the old ferry at Phetcharat Marina, situated on Ban Plai Laem, Koh Samui after a long and tiring journey from London. She chose not to get a connecting flight which could have compromised her ambiguity, which gave her the whole journey to try and understand how on earth Nastya's card had arrived at her door.

It was the afternoon and very hot, a discomfort which was overshadowed by the pungent smells wafting across from a large, sheltered street market. Old fish and rotting meat, in the heat, didn't seem to have any effect on the locals shopping. Lisa decided to erase this disturbing thought when sampling the local street food in the future, otherwise she could starve to death on Samui.

The market's presence ruined the pristine white beach, and it put Lisa off staying there. Instead, she decided to head to Big Buddha at the end of the beach and stay in some wooden huts that came recommended by her *Rough Guide to Thailand*. Big Buddha was on an island and accessed via a small road on a man-made 'spit', which divided the clear beautiful sea. Her journey took about fifteen minutes. She didn't find Big Buddha that impressive, but agreed he *was* big - and there, just below, she found the wooden bungalows. With ropey balconies that hung over the shallow turquoise waters, Lisa wondered about the night-time creepy crawly parties under the beds.

After she negotiated a price with the friendly Thai owner, he took her to the chosen accommodation. She agreed to pay extra for a fan and then after discarding her backpack on the floor, sat on a big chair overlooking the sea. She marvelled at the scenery where she could see another curved beach shaded by palms in the distance, deciding this was truly paradise - hotel luxuries couldn't beat this no matter how many gimmicks were on offer.

'What's the point', she continued in her mind, 'paying huge amounts to trap you in a hotel, only to neglect the exploration of the beauty outside – one may as well stay in a five-star walled hotel in the Bronx'. She then wondered if five-star luxury was in-fact a self-inflicted walled prison.

What Lisa didn't realise during her musings, was that she was within walking distance of Five Palms House.

Lisa wasn't sure where to start in the search for her friends, but what she did know was that under no circumstances should she cross Gerry. If she did, she would become another 'missing person'. She wasn't sure if he knew what she looked like, which influenced her decision to reduce her stay, figuring that the longer she stayed the more likely she'd be found.

What she had to go on to find Nastya was very basic and Five Palms House was out of bounds, an avenue shut down unless she went there with an army. She knew many answers lay there, but what could she do? Sneak in at night?

So, she had to concentrate on the strange hotel place on Chaweng Beach with a Martin Kunsmann, and Joe, an American also at Chaweng who dealt with water coolers. She had a plan to find the Amari company and see if they could direct her to Martin. And of course, there was always the hope that she may simply bump into the couple she was looking for in the first place. She also decided to check the airport for any flight plans they may have had or have. For all Lisa knew they could be on a plane back to the UK. Timmingham found out there was no information on them.

Lisa had worked out most of the details of the outrageously simple plan to relieve the West of its gold reserves by blackmail, and that Gerry and all his hornets on Samui were the perpetrators. She also understood, thanks to her father's cryptic message, that Gerry and a woman called Reklem were key protagonists of the plan - although Reklem appeared to live in Montenegro, near a place called Kotor.

This was an amazing coincidence as Lisa's father used to live in Ulcin, a small coastal town on the border of Montenegro and Albania.

Because of this, Lisa understood the bank account name she had discovered was Crne Gore (pronounced Chorne Gora). Translated in Serbian, it meant *Black Mountain*, which dominated the coastal lands of Montenegro (Monte Negro also translates as Black Mountain). Having Serbian set up on her computer's vocabulary probably opened a few doors that it shouldn't have. It must have been a password of sorts which had since been changed.

Lisa thought she'd try to track down Joe first – she'd concluded that an American selling water coolers in Koh Samui shouldn't be too hard to find. The next day she got on the trail and headed for Chaweng Beach. She decided to visit the hotels by day and bars by night. At an internet café she sent another message to Timmingham and gave the next rendezvous time.

She started at a Chaweng bar, breaking her own rule immediately. She sat on a high stool at a wooden table overlooking the street. The bar was called *Legends*. It had all the ingredients of being an untamed wild-west bar, and she imagined all the fun that happened there during the tropical nights. Her 'Rough Guide' explained that this place was a bit of an institution, just like the small *Ark Bar* across the road.

She watched scores of motorbikes navigate their way around the potholes filled with water from the previous night's rain. The masses of overhead telephone wires fascinated her, and she wondered how on earth you could repair an individual line should there be a fault, as there was no colour code – they were all black and tied together. There were hundreds of them tied resting on a post every 200 yards or so. She mused perhaps they were all defunct and didn't put it past the locals not to remove them.

She decided to make a move.

"Excuse me," said Lisa to the barmaid.

The barmaid looked as if she'd just done a twenty-four-hour shift and stared at Lisa vacantly.

"Do you have any water coolers?" Lisa asked, edging her way to the point.

The blank stare didn't flinch, so she continued. "I'm looking for a young guy called Joe, American" and before she could continue the waitress smiled.

"You in wrong place, we only have girls here lady," and she laughed.

"Yes, that's very funny, but seriously, I'm looking to find a guy called Joe who sells water coolers. It's important to me."

The waitress paused a moment then shouted into the dark shadows inside, "Any American water sellers called Joe?"

"No." replied a man's voice.

"No," conveyed the waitress.

Lisa gave a wry smile.

"Thank you...can I pay?"

"It doesn't get tougher than that," said Lisa to herself as she hopped off the stool and headed across the road to the *Ark Bar*.

Lisa sat once again, except this time with a sea view. A waiter came and she ordered a coffee. "Is the manager around?" she asked hesitantly. Surprisingly, she received an affirmative answer without any difficulty. The cool breeze blew through the shaded terrace and a man came over after a conversation with her waiter.

"Hi, I'm Terry Bouaris, the manager, can I help you?"

"You're Australian?"

"That's right. G'day mate!" said Terry, smiling broadly.

"Sorry, walked right into that," said Lisa, recognising her own tribe, thinking that his accent sounded like it was from Melbourne.

"Sure did mate," said Terry in an exaggerated Australian accent.

Lisa laughed and Terry sat opposite her and leant back on his chair.

"How long have you lived here?" said Lisa trying a different, less direct approach.

"Quite a few years. You here on holiday?"

"Sadly no, but I wish I lived here."

"So then, what's the mission?"

Lisa thought a moment, "I'm trying to find a missing friend."

Terry sat up, "Oh I'm sorry, is it serious?"

"I hope not, but my instincts say yes." Lisa then considered the incestuous nature of the island and changed tracks as Terry may well know Gerry - or be owned by him.

"Anyway, a friend of hers, Joe, will know of her whereabouts. He sells water coolers. You wouldn't know him by any chance, would you?"

"I actually do."

"You're joking, an American guy?"

"That's the one," said Terry, his suntanned, lined face adjusting to his smile.

For some reason Lisa felt she could trust Terry, but not just yet.

"He isn't around, is he?"

"No, I believe he just left briefly for Bangkok." Terry thought for a moment, "But maybe not. If he's here, he should be doing his rounds, heading towards Maenam Beach around now, I can find out for you".

"Oh, that would be amazing!" said Lisa.

"I'll make a call."

"Thank you. Who are you calling? Perhaps I could go and meet them?"

"P. Bun Ma, he's a local bar, club and hotel owner." said Terry, oblivious to Lisa's horror. "Kind of a big shot around here, he knows a lot of what goes on".

"P. Bun Ma, er, no. Wait!" and she put her hand on Terry's.

A pause ensued as Lisa had to fathom out a reason for why not to call him, without alerting Terry.

"You ok? Do you know him?" asked Terry, confused.

"No, I just realised something, I must go, I'm meant to meet someone. Now! Terry, can I call you back?"

"Sure, anytime, I'm always here or at this place." Terry gave Lisa a card showing P. Bun Ma's shop in Bang Rak.

"Thanks Terry, I'll call soon, I'm sorry I've got to break off like this, it clearly slipped my mind,". Terry could see she wasn't telling the truth and decided to keep it to himself, aware of the fact that P. Bun Ma was a dangerous man in the underworld and maybe Lisa didn't belong here. He wondered who it was that was missing.

"Do you live in Chaweng?" asked Lisa, readying herself to leave.

"No, Bang Rak, near Big Buddha." said Terry.

"I'm staying right below him," said Lisa a little surprised, "the wooden huts."

"I know the ones. Do you have a photo of your missing friend by the way? Pretty much everyone who comes to Samui passes through here at some point. I see most of them, it's my job."

Lisa felt obliged to show Terry a photo, as it would seem very odd to travel halfway around the globe without such an item. She pulled out the photo and could see that Terry had no idea who Nastya was.

"Nope. Don't recognise her. Striking girl! Very odd, as people can't resist the beach music, and we're the only ones really. Was she on holiday?"

"Sort of, why?"

"Well, if you went to Paris, you would visit the Eiffel Tower. Not saying we're the Eiffel Tower, but if you're having fun, this is where you'd come, so maybe she's left the island."

"Interesting point and noted."

Lisa by now couldn't get away fast enough, as for all she knew, P. Bun Ma may walk into the bar at any moment. She closed the conversation diplomatically and chose to relax for a while at a place she had heard about, and wanted to see, called *The Jungle Club*.

Terry realised once she left that she had never volunteered her name.

The Jungle Club was situated high above Chaweng on the side of a jungle-clad mountain. *'It sure is well named'*, she thought as she marvelled at the breathtaking views of beaches and coves stretching along Samui's east coast from the cantilevered decks. She could see Big Buddha in the distance, which appeared no more than the size of her thumbnail.

It was a strange place, as it was up a hill so steep that a special jeep was commissioned to take customers on the last part of the journey. She met some holiday makers in the back, and they all joked and laughed on what was essentially quite a scary ride. Once there, she sat alone on the giant bean bags that were positioned close to the edge of the deck. The drop on the other side was not to be trifled with as it would kill most. The Thai disregard for health and safety measures was clearly evident here.

Recognising both Lamai and Chaweng beaches below her starting to light up in the encroaching dusk, she noticed numerous fishing boats out on the horizon with their bright lights on to fool the fish below into their nets. Lisa now understood why there were no fish to be seen near the beaches, or on the reefs (a common complaint by visitors to the island), as there were about a hundred boats and the fishermen were going about decimating the lot, with no regard for the tourists. Times, she thought, were going to change for the tourist industry.

The cool mountain breeze played with Lisa's hair as she absorbed her perfect surroundings where nature, colour and temperature excited every sense in her body. Her concentration on this perfection was soon broken by the realisation that she was technically on the run and that she had better get off the island as soon as possible, before someone did it for her. She didn't want to consider the implications of not finding her friend Nastya, as the thought would be too hard for her to bear. She simply hoped Nastya had left the island with G.

Lisa wished she had a sign that Nastya was alright. As this thought ran through her mind, she was distracted by a curtain blowing in the wind on one of the nearby wooden dining salas, set apart from the main decks. It was blowing more than the other curtains, which were hanging almost motionless. It then occurred to her that the curtain was blowing *against* the wind and not with it which made no sense at all, then suddenly it stopped. Lisa said quietly to herself, "Nastya, is that you?" and sat up.

She looked around and all was normal. She ran through what had just happened once more in her mind. She sat back again and drank her cocktail. "If it's you," she said to herself, "and you're *not* ok, send another sign."

A white squirrel suddenly appeared, as if from nowhere, on the edge of the deck. It looked at Lisa and then jumped off. It was gone. Lisa put down her drink, got up and slowly walked to where the squirrel had been. She cautiously peered over the edge at the sheer drop. It was nowhere to be seen. Lisa stepped back and returned to her bean bag and slowly sipped her drink contemplating the ramifications of what she'd just witnessed. The rabbit in Alice in Wonderland registered in her mind, perhaps it was time to go!

***.

1999. The Stairs

Gunn was looking out to sea once more in this hazy slow-motion world. The sea, beach, muffled sound. He knew what awaited. The stairs. What was it down there? Once again, he wanted to resist but couldn't. He had no control, when suddenly things began to become more vivid as he slowly descended, then sounds became clearer. A cry of a seagull broke the stupor of the scene, and the waves could be heard clearly now. People behind him were talking and became more coherent - he slowly turned around.

"Whaaaa, te de where..." said Gunn incomprehensively, waking up in a sweat.

1999. Gerry's Worry

Gerry stood on his terrace by the lake, digesting what had just happened. Gerry felt his iron fist was loosening to events that seemed all a little too coincidental. He'd just killed four people, and now he had Sawa in the secret room as well!

He was getting edgy about P. Bun Ma, who would tell Reklem. Gerry couldn't believe the timing, as he'd only just explained to Reklem that all was well. He began to think it was time to return to the UK as something wasn't right in Thailand. More to the point, in his house! He then heard a whisper in the air which said, "That won't help."

Gerry stood motionless, only moving his eyes to their peripherals. Then slowly he looked around but all he could see was the guard at the main doors. He wondered if he'd heard anything at all - whatever it was had been barely audible, so, perhaps, he hoped, it was the wind.

Then he heard some footsteps walking across the bridge. He could see no one! His eyes widened to no avail as there was nothing to see. He shook his head in disbelief and walked past where he heard the footsteps, towards the guard, for reassurance - who saluted him.

"Hi," said Gerry, edgily looking over his shoulder. "Did you hear footsteps walking across the bridge.

"Steps?" said the Thai guard.

"Nothing, don't worry," said Gerry, realising the futility of his question.

The guard looked at Gerry and feeling him to be nervous, chose to say nothing more, fearing Gerry's temper.

"I'm going to stay in Bang Rak tonight. Can you help me get my things?".

This was a strange request thought the guard, obliged to help. Gerry went to his quarters with the guard following behind to get his things. The guard was now seeing a different side to Gerry, one he'd not seen before. He thought he saw fear in Gerry's eyes.

***.

1999. Missing Tourist

Gunn arrived at the scene of the accident on the Ghost Road. A parked police car gave away the exact location where a welcoming and familiar police officer strode towards Gunn to greet him.

"So, what's the problem now. Tam, isn't it?"

"Yes, well remembered."

The officer, Tam, explained and showed Gunn the dried blood on the road.

"It's still wet over there," said Gunn, pointing to some more blood. Tam looked over his shoulder and saw it. "Whatever happened, it's recent. Get a sample and find out what blood group it is. Or... maybe there's more than one source of blood. Different people?".

158

"Ok, Detective."

"No witnesses?" asked Gunn, distractedly looking for clues.

"No, only the voice that rang in, sounded American - and not from here. Maybe a tourist."

"Possibly," doubted Gunn. "Let me know if anyone reports any missing tourists."

"I will, of course," said Tam, who was aware of Gunn's reputation for forensics and his English connection.

"So, when did that call come in?"

"Er."

"Two hours, three...last night?" said Gunn impatiently, still thinking about Nurse Sawa.

"About three hours ago."

"Well, Tam," said Gunn, "The blood had dried out way before that judging by what I'm seeing, so that call was quite delayed. What took him so long I wonder?" Realising what he'd just said, Gunn paused. This particular scene, yet another one, had blood but no victims.

"There's a lot of missing people on this island," said Gunn out loud.

"What?" said Tam.

"Nothing," replied Gunn pensively. "Look, I want you to hang around here for the next few hours. If you see anything odd or anybody that might have seen anything, have a chat with them. Ask them if they've seen anything. Ok?"

"Ok," said Tam eagerly.

"How old are you?"

"Twenty-five."

Gunn smiled and put his hand on Tam's shoulder, like a father to a son, "Good luck, I bet you find something. Stay sharp. Be lucky," Gunn turned to leave as Tam saluted, before turning back with an after-thought.

"Sorry Tam, what did the American say exactly?"

"He said to come quickly, there had been an accident and that someone may have died. He said it was on the first turning off the Ghost Road by the airport."

"Any background sounds?"

Tam thought for a second, "No."

"Did he sound concerned?" asked Gunn.

"Afraid." was the surprising answer. "Now you mention it, it sounded like he was being told what to say."

Gunn took this in and asked no further questions.

1999. Circles

Gunn was sleeping restlessly and then woke up suddenly with his eyes wide open. He realised that a lot was going on which may be connected. He stared at the ceiling a while longer and got up after contemplating the scenarios. It was about three in the afternoon, the usual time he slept for an hour. He pulled back the curtains and turned off the air conditioning, then made himself a coffee.

He sat on the large colonial styled terrace in an armchair and stared at the sea, whilst sipping from the cup. The sea was magnificent and for once there was a sea breeze. His mind was clearing.

He decided to implement the six-handshake rule which he had read about and consider if all this recent activity *was* connected. Coincidence is the undoing of many a plot – this was Gunn's philosophy in solving crimes, where the ridiculous somehow made sense.

He got up and went to his whiteboard in the office next to the living room.

He drew some circles with numbers and wrote:

No 1. '2 missing bodies, P. Bun Ma, Five Palms House?'

No 2. 'Keys. 2 coma people. Nurse Sawa. Doctor Smith'.

He drew another circle, and this was the odd one,

No 3. 'Man missing, car crash, missing body?'

He stood back and stared at the board a while. He put on a crisp white shirt whilst doing so and rolled his sleeves up exposing his expensive brushed steel, Hamilton watch. He prided himself on his appearance and always stood out. His mix of Thai and English made him look like a Westerner with a permanent tan, of which he was quite proud - *the package,* which didn't tally with most people's conception of what a detective should look like. He also remembered his mother Dorothy, teasing him saying, 'You might not be the dumbest guy in the world, but you sure better hope he doesn't die'.

He smiled to himself as he pondered a connection between the three circles. The two missing bodies, he mused, had to be a red herring, and not related to the two coma patients. The timings didn't add up. Gunn was faced with the scenario of two *walking dead*, two missing dead, another missing dead, and another missing. He wished he could just talk to someone - *before* they went missing. Samui was living up to its reputation as the 'Island of Ghosts'.

The phone rang, it was Tam. He told Gunn he spoke to the 'American' who was in fact a Thai street seller with a mobile cooking unit. He 'caught' him whilst he was setting up his BBQ by the mystery scene. This was pretty much what Gunn had assumed.

"I asked if he was there last night, and he confirmed. I recognised the accent. His wife said she didn't want him to call the police. Here's the thing though, there were *three cars* involved."

"I'm listening," said Gunn without emotion. "Carry on."

"Oh sorry," said Tam, "there was a collision, and a girl was killed. The damaged car drove off. The other two cars did the same, one with a door missing. This is the weird part though, the third car returned and cleared up the scene, taking the body and door. The car's occupants didn't see the informant; hence he's scared. I'm surprised he turned up today at all. Guess he needs the money."

"Did he get a look at any of the people...a dead girl you say."

"No," said Tam. "He said it was too dark."

"Bring him in."

"Ok boss."

Gunn added the new information to a circle on the board. He realised this *now* could indeed be connected.

Then a shiver went down his spine as he saw that the name Nurse Sawa had moved from circle 1 - to circle 3 on the board.

"Tam, you have the results of the blood on the street?"

"I do, although I don't understand what they will prove."

"Just give me the results Tam, I have a theory."

"Sorry boss, AB blood group."

"Really. Now that *is* interesting."

"Why?"

"It's a very rare blood group."

"Ok. Er - talk you later."

Gunn went across Nathon Town to the hospital, a fifteen-minute walk which gave him time to 'square the peg' in the round hole. '*How on Earth did that writing move in the circles on the board*' he thought perplexedly. It just made no sense to him.

"Doctor Smith thank you for seeing me, did you get what I asked for?"

"Yes Gunn, but what a strange request!"

"Have you seen her at all? I bet not," said Gunn.

"Actually no. I haven't."

"So, what's the score?

"AB *is* Sawa's blood group. How did you know? Is this important?" said Doctor Smith.

Gunn sat down and looked at the floor and thought about circles.

1999. Missing Sawa

At Nathon, Doctor Jah was very concerned about her missing friend Nurse Sawa. Sawa had told her of a very important key hidden in her chair. She said that if she were to disappear, the key could save her life – as it could be used as a bargaining chip.

Doctor Jah had waited a few days now. If Sawa didn't show up soon, Doctor Jah understood she would have to retrieve the key quickly, in case they replaced her chair. Something Doctor Jah noticed since Sawa's disappearance was that a man had been in her line of vision a couple of times over the last few of days. A man she didn't know and who certainly wasn't a patient, as she was a gynaecologist. Her surgery was a five-minute drive from Nathon Hospital, and she finally decided it prudent to go and find the key. As a precaution, she picked up the phone and once again asked Doctor Smith if he had any idea of Sawa's whereabouts.

He said he did not, so she asked if she could meet with him, to which he agreed. She requested to meet at the hospital and look through Nurse Sawa's office, lying about the true reason. Again, Doctor Smith agreed, and they set a time for the next day.

"Who was that?" asked Detective Gunn, who was still sitting down trying to absorb the new blood information. Gunn had picked up on the concern in Doctor Smith's voice.

"Funnily enough, Doctor Jah, a friend of Nurse Sawa."

"Fancy that?" said Gunn, "and she wants to look around her office…for what?"

"No idea. We'll see tomorrow I guess."

"Don't tell her about me, will you?" said Gunn looking pointedly at Doctor Smith.

"Sure, no. No, I won't."

"Thank you," said Gunn. "I have my reasons."

Later that evening Gunn added Doctor Jah to Nurse Sawa in circle 3.

1999. Stay Alive!

Gunn was up early, he felt this was going to be a big day. He decided to check up on Doctor Jah and drove to her surgery, which wasn't anything special but was up to date and modern. It still stood out amongst the neighbouring wooden shacks, that sat around the small muddy yard, which was currently for parking. Beyond this was a grubby river where humans had yet again managed to ruin nature's jungle beauty.

'Do we really belong on this planet?' contemplated Gunn as he surveyed the disappointing area. *'We turn beauty into brown. Green into brown. We eat beautiful things and turn them into brown too! If you were in space looking down and saw brown...that's where you'd find humans.'* Gunn smiled at this abysmal thought. He nodded his head to himself and then noticed a man in a car across the car park. The man wasn't doing much, just sitting there, and hadn't noticed Gunn. Gunn watched him for a while and decided the man was watching Jah's surgery. This now shored things up in Gunn's mind that something big was going on, and it centred around the missing key. He now had a choice – stay low and risk another missing witness or confront the suspects.

The latter would most certainly bring him into direct conflict with P. Bun Ma, as Gunn *knew* he was involved. Involved with precisely what, he didn't know. He watched as the man in the car received a phone call before hurriedly driving off. Gunn started his engine and decided on the spot to follow. It was raining and quite misty, with the clouds descending from the mountains through the dense foliage.

The man headed towards Chaweng and Gunn found himself, once again, on a journey down his least favourite piece of coastal road. By now, due to the island's notoriously poor drainage, it was starting to flood. It was close to the monsoon season where the rains isolated entire areas as the rivers burst their restraints. This downpour he thought, could be the beginning. Thanks to these conditions, the car ahead would have obscured rear vision, which suited him nicely as they neared the Big C supermarket – Gunn would remain undetected.

Suddenly the car ahead turned sharply, cutting across the path of an oncoming car, causing its annoyed driver to press hard and long on his horn. Gunn couldn't follow as he would have had a head-on collision if he'd have tried. He continued along the road cursing, as he caught a glance of the suspect disappearing into the distance down a narrow banana shaded alley. "Fuck, fuck, fuck!" shouted Gunn in his damp, enclosed space, before deciding to check in with Tam.

"Hey Boss." Tam answered.

"Hi Tam. I don't have much time to talk. You know Doctor Jah?"

"Yes."

"Follow her...now!" said Gunn forcefully.

"But I'm waiting for the street seller, he's just about to come!"

"Shit...then get officer Kla (Thai for brave man) to deal with him. You go find Doctor Jah before she's dead." Gunn decided drama was the best way to get an immediate response, which was exactly the kind of response he wanted.

"Sure," said Tam, clearly shaken.

"Sorry, just be quick, that's all. I have to go."

"Ok."

It was too far now for Gunn to follow Doctor Jah, so he decided to calm down and have a coffee while letting his soldiers operate. With a sudden thought, Gunn rang Tam back.

"Boss?"

"Be discreet...very discreet. Ok? A life could be at stake, remember that."

Tam nodded his head as he was leaving the building and put the phone away. The rain was picking up as Tam got into the car to head towards Doctor Jah's.

Gunn proceeded to a very soggy Chaweng High Street. He parked in a hotel car park which he knew, and ended up in the Ark Bar hoping the rain would stop soon.

Gunn sat at a table by the sea.

"What can I get you sir?" said Terry.

1999. Leaving Samui

Lisa hurriedly packed her bags the next morning to catch the same ferry she had arrived on. The departure staff were infuriating but the boarding staff amazing. They somehow knew every bag and who it belonged to upon departure at Surat Thani, even though they were piled up indiscriminately in a pile. Lisa had had some bad news which now messed up her plan; her mother was in hospital having had a stroke. She lived in Corfu, which was an extremely long and difficult journey from Bangkok. It seemed that the Greeks considered their own paradise to be good enough, so there were no direct flights.

After the second harrowing journey in a month, Lisa got a taxi to the Greek hospital. Her mother was stable, but not really aware of who Lisa was when she arrived. She had respiratory aid and was on a drip, it was heart-wrenching for Lisa to see such deterioration in her closest friend. After much consolation from the nurses, she was persuaded to rest and return the next day.

After the usual desperate questions had been parried, they said the outcome was 50/50, which Lisa took to mean hopeless. She got her bags, defeated, and headed to Gouveia Marina where her deceased father's boat lay idle. She was a 43DS Jeanneau, Sun Odyssey, and beautiful - named Lady Marie D.

It was dark, silent and warm, with all the other yachts silhouetted in the half-moon light. She was almost opposite the entrance and Lisa easily found the yacht, which took her breath away. It felt extremely odd for her to get onboard, as she hadn't been on since it was brought over from Vietnam. It was, in Lisa's eyes, still a murder scene which she hoped to solve sometime soon.

She threw her bags into the cockpit and clambered aboard. Lady M still had her magic she thought, getting the galley door keys out of her bag. She opened them - and the smell inside was wonderful. Lisa loved yachts and the smells and noises that went with them, although the *fun* element rapidly disappeared as she looked down into the dark, moonlit galley. There, at the bottom of the stairs she imagined her dead father lying. She paused with this thought for some time before descending, stepping over, through respect, where he would have been.

She put her hands on the kitchen work bench directly in front of the stairs, leant forward, and began to cry. She sobbed uncontrollably on her own with no one around for consolation as she contemplated her mother's, father's and now possibly Nastya's mortality. For the first time in ages, she felt weak and isolated, surrounded by potential assassins. She pulled out her phone and did something she shouldn't have done.

1999. "I love you"

Julian was lying on his bed thinking about life and Lisa. He thought of her every day and wondered if she would ever call again. His phone, which he left on the hall table, suddenly rang.

"Shit," he said to himself as he hauled himself off the bed. He walked casually to the ringing phone and then it stopped.

"Fucking hell, what is this?" Missed call appeared on his phone. He started to try and find the unidentified number on his past calls when it suddenly rang again.

"Hello?"

The caller remained silent.

"Lisa. That's you, isn't it? Hello Lisa?"

"Julian, how did you know?"

Julian practically sank to his knees. "Oh my God, I've missed you so much...are you ok? Where are you?"

Lisa sniffled, "I'm fine, I'm in Corfu. I've been to Thailand..."

"I love you Lisa, I can't stop thinking about you."

"You've no idea, I love you too."

They both felt silent for a moment, absorbing all this new information.

"I've loved you a long time," then she laughed.

"What?"

"They say that in Thailand." said Lisa, wiping her nose. "You're not going to believe this, but I've literally just got back from there."

Julian took a seat by the window where he could see a sunset in its last stages.

"I've only met you once and I fell in love with you. You must be something special."

Lisa laughed, "I am."

"The keys to my flat. How on earth did you pull off that trick?

"I'll tell you another time. Listen." Silence.

Yes?

I don't know where to start," Lisa giggled. "Ok I've been watching you for years, I figured that you'd put the two notes together and worked that out.

"I did!" said Julian euphorically. "It *was* you. Oh my God, what's going on?"

"Knowing me is dangerous, I don't know if you know that? It's a risk talking to you even now, but I just needed to hear your voice. I've missed you so much. I really did," and Lisa started to weep.

"When can we see each other again?"

"Come to Corfu," said Lisa off the cuff.

"What?"

"Yes come. Can you?"

"You bet," said Julian. "I'll be there tomorrow."

"Do that and get a new phone. Leave your one there. Put it on divert."

"Sure. Where do I find you?"

Lisa decided to play a bit with Julian. "On a yacht."

Julian cocked his head. "A... yacht? I love a girl with a yacht? Boy am I good at choosing my girls. Where?"

"I'll be brief - I don't know if your phone is tapped. Call me from your new phone and I'll tell you where. Tomorrow?"

"Tomorrow. I got your number." said Julian.

"Love you."

"I love you too."

1999. Corfu

Julian got on the internet straight away and found a flight from Gatwick leaving at 10am the next morning. He booked it and then attempted to sleep after packing a small backpack. Julian had some information too, and presumed he knew more than Lisa realised.

The next morning he was early for the train from Hampton Wick station. On the way out he bumped into his neighbours.

"Hi Julian." said Ali, holding her daughter Matilda's hand and carrying their newborn, Jaimie.

"Morning. Morning Mark."

"Where you off to, holidays?" asked Mark.

"Off to meet the love of my life."

"I didn't realise," said Ali. "How long's this been going on for?" she asked cheekily. "Have you been sneaking her in?"

"I've only met her once."

Mark and Ali looked at each other and smiled. "Ok," said Mark sarcastically.

"It's a long story, I'll tell you about it another time, but I'm off to see her now."

"Where?"

"Between you and me... and keep it to yourself. Seriously. Corfu. I've known her for years. Apparently," and Julian smiled wryly to himself. "Look, I have to go. I've a flight to catch."

"Sure. Bon voyage," said Mark and Matilda did a little wave as Julian began to leave.

"When are you back?" shouted Ali.

"Dunno, see you soon!" and Julian disappeared.

172

1999. Scared

Gerry decided he wanted to be with people, or at least be surrounded by them, so he chose a small coastal hotel close to the 'Fisherman's Village' sign in Bophut. His guard dropped Gerry's bags off at his room and went back to Five Palms House, confused as to why he would give up that luxury for a hotel room.

Gerry walked past the T- junction towards the other end of Bophut beach to a bar he liked called Gecko. He loved the music they played, and the staff were very pleasant. He sat on a beach sala and tried to absorb what was going on. Life, he contemplated, had mostly been a breeze yet something very strange had now taken hold. He worked out that he was actually scared of his own house and wondered if it had anything to do with the bodies in the hidden room under the library.

He had no doubt that he'd heard the footsteps, and... possibly the voice - but what he couldn't understand was what happened when he was interrogating Nurse Sawa. He could still visualize the right side of her face turning blue, and the condensation normally associated with warm breath coming into contact with freezing air. Was the house haunted, he wondered – a ridiculous thought as he didn't believe in that sort of thing.

He switched tracks and came back to the key. He still didn't have it, and he needed to get the information from the box at Siam Bank as soon as possible. He couldn't use force on the manageress Ming, as she had a distant connection to the Prime Minister. If he messed with her, not even P. Bun Ma could save him. If he burnt the place down, it may still not reveal the contents... if they survived. If he got that information, he could get rid of Reklem, who he never had liked. He also didn't trust her, but Reklem had the second key to gain access, and he had now lost his.

She was too 'Soviet' in his eyes, which meant to him that her loyalties probably lay elsewhere. He felt that there were too many strange bedfellows, none of whom had loyalty to each other. Revenge and hate seemed to be the only common thread between them all, which didn't bode well as Gerry felt the plot was only as strong as its weakest link, which summed up almost everyone concerned.

He'd found out that a certain Doctor Jah was Sawa's best friend and could possibly know where Sawa hid the key, but the tag he placed on her, so far, had revealed nothing. If Reklem found out he'd lost the key, he wasn't sure what the consequences would be. Death couldn't be ruled out.

Gerry breathed out and listened to a track he loved by Tracy Chapman, ironically called 'Bang, Bang, Bang'. He had to smile at that, although deep down he was shattered, as he hadn't signed up to being a mass murderer. He ordered another drink and began to realise he was losing the plot a bit, so he made a decision to get away from the island for a while and return to London – to let things settle.

Besides, he mused, he *was* afraid of his own house. He looked away from the sea and saw a girl in the distance - in the shadows – in the table by the bushes, looking at him. The girl didn't seem right then he realised why. She had *that* red hair.

1999. Coincidence

Gunn was sitting with his back to Terry and didn't really notice him when he ordered a coffee. Terry gave the order to a waiter who brought the coffee to Gunn's table. Gunn answered his phone, "Hi Tam, what you got?"

"She's still in her surgery."

"Thank God. Anything else? Anybody suspicious?

"No just a bunch of mothers, girls going in for their pregnancy check-ups I guess."

"OK good. If anyone suspicious goes near her, step in. I think she knows something others want to find out about. I'll be with you in about an hour. She has an appointment with Doctor Smith at 3pm so I'll be keeping an eye on that."

"Ok boss, oh, what was that all about with the blood sample?"

"I think it belonged to Nurse Sawa."

Tam went silent then said "Sawa. What, so she's dead?"

"I think she is. She's missing, that's for sure, her apartment has been abandoned. She knew about this key which everyone wants. So yes. I think she got in the way of something."

"Wow," said Tam unquestioningly. "Ok. I'll see you soon."

***

"Detective Gunn?"

"Yes," said Gunn turning around.

"I thought so, Terry, P. Bun Ma remember?" Terry shook Gunn's hand.

"Of course, how are you? You work here?"

"Yes, P. Bun Ma sends me here in the day and early evenings. Nice weather, eh?"

"Yes lovely. Looks like the monsoon's coming early."

"I reckon so. What brings you here? Missing people?" asked Terry grinning, unaware at the effect that such an innocent question would have on Gunn.

Gunn stared at Terry a moment, wondering if that was a loaded question or a throw-away comment, before replying, "Always looking for something. You have anyone in mind?"

"Well oddly, yes," said Terry, with a conspiratorial look on his face as he pulled up a chair and sat on it, back to front, resting his arms on the backrest. "A girl came in looking for someone. She freaked out when I mentioned P. Bun Ma."

The rain was now coming down really hard, to the point that Gunn could hardly hear. It flattened the waves as they approached the shore ahead of him, making them look like they were wading through treacle. The humidity remained thick.

"Who was looking for who?", shouted Gunn above the din.

"A blond girl looking for her friend from London. She showed me a photo. She was pretty, the friend... had red hair."

Gunn sat down again. "What kind of red hair?"

"Shaped in a bob, unmistakeable."

This information was beginning to overload Gunn. He couldn't stop coming across missing people! He had an inkling that this was the same girl he had seen on the beach with her friends, who had been interested in Gerry Absalom's land. After all, how many girls do you come across with bright red bobs?

"This blond," he continued, "she knew P. Bun Ma?"

"Judging by her reaction, it seemed that way. She tried to shut down the conversation."

"Did she say if this girl went missing recently?"

"Sounded that way, I reckon within the last month, the way she was talking. She's staying by Big Buddha. The wooden huts there."

"Really?" said Gunn, realising he was getting late for Doctor Smith. "I'll check it out."

"Sure," said Terry.

"Do you know her?" asked Terry, realising Gunn's interest.

"Not sure, but gotta go, I'm late, I'll let you know!" Gunn cowed as he ran into the rain heading back to his car.

***

1999. Time to get out!

Gerry stared at the girl with red hair and realised she wasn't who he thought she was, and that she was staring at a yacht coming into Bo Phut Bay - behind Gerry. The girl swapped seats with her friend to avoid Gerry's stare, which embarrassed him. Gerry shook his head disappointed at his own paranoia and went to pay his bill.

The next morning after a restless sleep he made immediate plans to return to London. He didn't want to come back! His staff would send his stuff the next day and he took a separate, hastily packed suitcase to the airport. He couldn't bring himself to tell Reklem, as he'd had quite a rough time over the past few days and a good ear-chewing was the last thing he needed right now. Before he'd left the house, he looked around the gardens standing by the gates. He no longer felt welcome, but by whom, he pondered. Or what?

1999. Lady Marie D

Julian arrived at the airport and found a shop selling pay-as-you-go phones. After fiddling around with the sim-cards and payments, he finally got it working, dialled out and Lisa answered immediately.

"Honey I'm home."

Lisa laughed. "Get your butt down to Gouveia Marina ASAP. It's about twenty minutes in the taxi. I'll meet you at reception. The yacht's called Lady Marie D, in case we miss each other."

"Message understood," and Julian hung up.

The taxi ride thrilled Julian, it was one of his favourite things in life – hurtling to a paradise destination with the taxi window open and the wind piling through his hair. It was a form of foreplay. However, now he couldn't think of anything that could beat Lisa riding on top of him. The sun was shining and everything was vivid. Julian felt invincible as the taxi pulled into the marina. Lisa was there with the biggest smile Julian had ever seen, he gave the taxi driver a huge note and didn't wait for the change. The driver got the message and hurriedly got Julian's backpack out of the boot.

Lisa grabbed Julian and they kissed forever. "Get a room," quipped Julian. Lisa didn't answer and pulled Julian behind her towards the pontoon where the Lady M lay. Julian looked in awe at the yacht and Lisa gave him a moment to do so, before manhandling him on-board, desperate for the long-awaited sex she was craving. She paused at the gangway thinking of her father and where he had lain, but passion got the better of her and she introduced Julian to the rear master cabin.

She didn't let him out for two hours. A couple walking past on the jetty could easily hear Lisa's moans of ecstasy and commented on the merits of having a yacht.

Finally, with their appetites sated, Lisa made Julian a coffee whilst he sat in heaven in the rear cockpit. He couldn't quite believe his luck.

"So, let's talk," said Julian breaking the silence as Lisa handed him his coffee. He put his arm around her. "What were you doing following me?"

 Lisa went on to explain the story.

"Gerry. I don't get this bit. Was that a set up?

"Not sure," said Lisa.

"He lived where I lived in Cheyne Court, which was amazing!"

"That was a lie, they know all about you. He never lived there."

"So..." and Julian stopped to take on board all the deception and set ups.

"This isn't a set-up, is it?" asked Julian, half joking.

"No, Julian it isn't, on that you can trust me." She thought for a moment. "How's Nick?"

"He's fine. Can't find Nastya, who was going to lead me to you."

"Funny you should say that, it's why I was in Thailand."

"Really?"

"Nastya's missing." Lisa went quiet and became pensive. She breathed in, "I think she's come across Gerry...well she *has* come across Gerry, but I don't think she got away. I think she's dead."

This was big information for Julian who said nothing.

"She sent me a weird note," and Lisa went on to describe events including the mystery voice in her Clapham house.

"Shit, are you sure? Dead?"

"No, but it makes sense. There were no flights back with...ah!" Lisa paused at a realisation, "G will be dead too, as they were together."

Julian was again speechless. He felt that just one sentence from all the information he'd just received would have been enough for most, for a year.

"You're not going to believe this," said Julian.

"What?"

"Well, if someone is killed, you'd presume the police would be involved, right?"

"Go on."

"If there were any bodies, they'd know."

"So.."

"I may know a detective on Koh Samui. In a place called, what was it? Nathon, I think."

Lisa looked at Julian, not fully understanding where this was leading. "What are you talking about?" she asked.

"Many years ago, I met a young guy in a pub in Chelsea, and, well he said he was studying forensics for the police, and that he would be stationed at Nathon, and to look him up."

Lisa smiled, "That's amazing, you don't remember his name, do you?"

"It was unforgettable. Gunn."

1999. Doctor Jah and Doctor Smith

Gunn arrived back at Doctor Jah's and saw that Tam's car was still there. Gunn drove on so as not to raise suspicion, should there be any hostile prying eyes around. He rang Tam.

"I'm here - what's going on?"

"Not much, but one car did pass by and linger. It had a male driver. I felt he was checking on Jah."

Gunn's windscreen wipers were on full tilt as the rain hadn't abated, he was about to speak when Doctor Jah emerged from the surgery with an umbrella. She scurried to her car.

"You got that Tam?"

"Got it."

"Follow me."

"Ok."

Doctor Jah drove off towards Nathon Hospital. This time Gunn didn't rely on the rain for concealment and followed at a two-car distance behind. As predicted, she drove into the hospital car park and pulled into a spot opposite the emergency entrance. The beach was obscured now by the driving grey rain. Gunn rang Doctor Smith.

"She's here...with you any minute now. She's looking for a key I think."

"A key?"

"Yes, you know the one.... Siam Bank.

"You're kidding."

"No time to explain. See if she finds it. Her life may depend on your findings."

"No pressure there, Gunn. Cheers, I'll do what I can." Doctor Smith hung up.

***

"Doctor Jah how are you?"

"I'm fine, Doctor Smith. Any news from Sawa? None I suppose," said Doctor Jah, answering her own question. Doctor Smith confirmed. Doctor Jah shook her head and looked sad.

"May I go in? I'm looking for a letter from her son; to get his address so I can write to him. Let him know. Maybe he knows."

"Good idea. Of course, be my guest. I'll come with you."

"No." said Doctor Jah, a little too suddenly. "Do you mind if I look alone?"

To insist would raise suspicion, so he said, "Go ahead. I hope you find it."

"Sure, thank you."

"You know the way." said Doctor Smith and sat down behind his desk. He rang Gunn.

"She's inside looking for a letter she said."

"I bet," said Gunn sarcastically. "I take it she didn't want you to go with her."

"She was quite insistent."

"Ok."

Doctor Jah closed the door to Sawa's office and saw the chair. She checked around and then began to feel around the small black leather chair. There it was. Under the seat cushion, lodged tightly between the glue. It pushed further in when Doctor Jah tried to prise it out.

"Shit."

She looked through the desk drawer and found a letter opener. To get the key would mean slightly tearing the cushion away. She had no choice. She got the key. She wondered if this was worth a life as she looked at the key up close. She flattened the front of her skirt down and left.

"Any luck?" asked Doctor Smith, looking up.

"No but thank you."

"Oh, sorry to hear that. We have details somewhere on her relatives but were waiting to see if she returned."

"Oh right. Could you let me have those please?"

Doctor Jah had lied, as she knew everything about Sawa. They had grown up together after Doctor Jah moved to Koh Ngai in the Malacca Straits, a tiny paradise island with only a few families inhabiting it. Most contact with humanity was provided by the few tourist ferries arriving either from Krabi or Langkawi, just over the Malay border to the north. For some bizarre reason this jewel in the crown had been generally overlooked by the tourists.

Doctor Jah got into her car and drove - followed by Gunn. Tam, by now, was inside seeing what Doctor Jah had been up to.

"It was in the chair. Or something was," he reported back to Gunn.

"Got it. I'll drive back to you when she stops."

As he drove slowly through the flooded streets and the rain, Gunn got a call.

"Hello?"

"Hi, is that Detective Gunn?" asked a voice in an English accent.

"Yes. Who's this?"

"I met you many years ago at a pub in Chelsea, London. My name is Julian."

***

"Julian. You shook my hand at the bar. I called you the 'Loaded Gunn'."

"Oh my God, I *do* remember you...and I miss the snow. What on earth, how did you get my number?"

184

"You said you'd probably be in Nathon."

"I did... amazing! That's a memory. You believed my prediction... So, are you looking for a free holiday?" asked Gunn laughing, realising he hadn't laughed in a while. He almost forgot what it was like and perhaps, he thought, he needed to take a break.

"Very funny, no... well yes, perhaps we can talk about that later," joked Julian. Lisa frowned and gestured to Julian to get on with it.

"Er, look this is a weird one but a friend of mine has gone missing,"

"Missing" repeated Gunn dryly and thought to himself *'how many more.... now people are ringing me from the other side of the world to tell me about missing people'*.

"Hello?"

"Sorry still here, who's the missing person?" asked Gunn wearily. Distracted and realising he hadn't slept properly for a while, he tried to find a parking spot to pull in to.

"She's got red hair. In a bob, she's young, pretty..."

"You're having me on," interrupted Gunn in disbelief, stopping the car in the middle of the sodden road. Cars beeped behind him.

"No, why would I? She's, well... my friend and I'm worried for her."

"Do you have a blonde girlfriend?" asked Gunn.

Confused by the 'out of the blue' question, Julian pulled the phone away from his ear and Lisa shook her head madly, mouthing, 'No!'

"No, why do you ask?" replied Julian, wavering after the prompt.

"Just wondering," said Gunn, disbelieving that Julian had no connection to the girl he'd heard about from Terry.

"No, I've not had any red-haired girls turn up in the morgue or reported missing."

Taken aback by Gunn's bluntness, Julian looked at Lisa. She implied hanging up.

"Can you help?"

I can try, but how?" Gunn was playing very cool. "Are you in Thailand, or planning on coming?"

"No, I..." and Lisa cut the phone off after taking it from Julian's hand.

Gunn looked at the phone, then put it on the passenger seat before driving off while giving a 'V' sign to the cars piled up behind him.

**

"Tam where is she?" asked Gunn.

"Back at the surgery. What shall we do?"

Gunn thought a moment. He decided to make a move instead of waiting to deal with yet another missing person file.

"Get one of the female officers in plain clothes down and bring her in. Pretend she's a patient, you understand?"

"I understand, I'll get on it now."

"Watch her like a hawk."

"Trust me boss." and Tam put the phone down. He then organised for a female colleague to come before getting out of his car, leaving his partner there to watch. "Back in a minute," he said.

The rain was easing up by now as he walked past the surgery. He went around the back and to his surprise, saw a large man about to go in through the rear door.

"Hey!" Tam shouted, and the man ran off. If the man had decided to confront Tam, Tam would have lost, he simply wasn't big enough. He followed at a steady running pace a safe distance behind, which clearly annoyed the man. They ran out from the jungle and back into the car park. Tam's partner immediately saw what was going on and got out of the police car to assist.

Doctor Jah also saw what was going on and went the opposite way, afraid of something happening to her, but unaware of what was really going on.

The man ran towards the river and suddenly fell. The two officers caught up with him and stared down. He wasn't moving and he had a bad wound on the back of his head. Tam knelt down and pushed the man so his face could be seen. He was dead, blood starting to trickle from a shot in the head, the wound behind was his brains. They quickly looked up and ran for cover.

"Doctor Jah, SHIT!!" shouted Tam and broke cover, potentially risking his life.

He ran back to the surgery, leaving his colleague to cover and make the unpleasant call to Gunn about the man.

Doctor Jah was gone! The back door was open.

***

Gunn sat at his desk and propped his head up with intertwined clenched fingers. He couldn't believe what was going on. What bothered him most was that in reality, he had absolutely *no* idea what was going on. There was too much information. He likened it to starting several books at once and only reading the first chapters of each whilst trying to work out endings. He doubted any of the books had happy endings, which made him smile with irony, as that was the opposite philosophy of the island.

He sighed, then got up and added another circle to the whiteboard, erasing Doctor Jah from circle 3 and creating a new circle 4, just for her, as she was now missing. Gunn kicked the bin as he went past it to make a coffee. He came back and added the dead assailant to Doctor Jah's circle. His next lead he decided was to find the blonde girl in the wooden huts at the base of Big Buddha. He hovered over the whiteboard for a moment but decided not to add circle 5 for the red-haired girl.

***

"Terry, did the blonde girl give you her name?"

"Sorry, no, Gunn. I realised after she left."

"That's no surprise...ok cheers. I'll keep in touch."

***

Gunn was back on his *favourite* road and contemplated moving to save journeying it again. He didn't smile at this sarcastic thought as he was angry at not getting a break. The population of Samui was being reduced dramatically and he wondered what level it would need to go down to, before he found *someone* that could actually tell him something.

He honked his horn furiously as two motorcyclists decided to ride side by side in the middle of the narrow road, not allowing him to pass. What really drove him mad was the trend where one motorcyclist put his foot on the neighbouring bike, which was now the case. He felt like arresting them on the charge of 'Stupidity'. It was their lucky day though, and he just overtook in the most aggressive way possible - almost running them off the road. The 'Sawa' circle really bothered Gunn. The moving name was inexplicable. He felt as if he were being led by something...Julian ringing out the blue after years about a redhead - bumping into Terry - again the redhead. Meeting the redhead on the beach that day.

With a sudden shock, he realised the girl with the red hair had been in the Christmas pub when he met Julian. She had been sitting behind him! Realising he needed a moment, he stopped the car, got out and walked along the beach which ran adjacent to the road. The sand was wet from all the rain, but he sat down nonetheless. He stared across the sea to Koh Phangan which was shrouded in mist.

"Surely...no surely, surely not. Julian couldn't have known the red-haired girl from back then, could he? They were separate and he met another man at the bar. So, a blonde girl who is probably Julian's girlfriend knows the red-haired girl... just not back then. Gunn simply couldn't work this out, it made no sense unless he added his favourite ingredient – coincidence. He would then be dealing with a very old coincidence! He stood up and wiped the wet sand off his bottom.

He got back into the car and continued to drive but was very distracted. "I'm going to need another fucking whiteboard," he said to himself. The sun started to break through the big black clouds. The monsoon was all or nothing at this point, which confused the tourists who used the deluges as an excuse to consume large amounts of alcohol as there was not much else to do. As Gunn approached Big Buddha, he thought of P. Bun Ma.

He parked in the dusty clearing nearby and got out of the car. *'Is he somehow involved in all this?'*, he wondered. This led Gunn's mind to that guy called Gerry, the Englishman who was simmering at Five Palms House. He shook his head as he asked himself "What for, why would all this stuff happen? There's no physical link. Why such an elaborate web?".

"Sorry?" said a tourist.

"I'm talking to myself, can't you see?" replied Gunn as he gave the tourist a cheesy grin.

"Sorry to ruin your conversation," retorted the tourist. Gunn's return stare made sure the tourist said no more. He walked to the wooden huts at the base of Big Buddha, which were drying out in the now hot sunshine, and went into the small section with a tourist restaurant and accommodation behind.

He walked into the reception area of the huts and was greeted with a "Sawasdee krup."

"Detective Gunn, do you have a moment?" said Gunn in Thai.

***

"I'm looking for a girl that I believed stayed here" said Gunn and went on to describe Lisa.

"Ah yes, I think I know," said the proprietor before disappearing through an open doorway adorned with hanging beads. He came back out and asked, "This girl?" He looked at the piece of paper in his hand which had her details on it. He continued, "Lisa Engles, British. She left very quickly."

"At last, a lead to someone that's not dead...yet." said Gunn somewhat morbidly.

Gunn immediately worked out that he could find out where Lisa had gone as he now had her passport number. He went back to the police station in a better mood, for he now had some hope. He was going to find out all about this Lisa Engles - or so he thought.

***

1999. Safety!

Young tourists hurried to and fro around the piers, looking for the right ferries to take them to yet another destination in their newly discovered paradise. Krabi tourism was beginning to boom, and the millennium was just on the horizon. Many here had decided to celebrate it in this Utopia. A small ferry pulled off with just a handful of tourists, on a journey which Doctor Jah knew well. The two-hour trip passed innumerable beautiful limestone islands with sheer cliff faces, making them uninhabitable. The seas surrounding them were crystal clear, turquoise and deep. As the ferry navigated its way through this marine paradise, the tourists sunbathed and looked in amazement as the fantastic scenery unrelentingly revealing more and more of its idyllic features.

Doctor Jah was heading for Kuantoang Bay on Koh Ngai, where she had spent much of her childhood with her buddy, Sawa. Here she felt she would be safe, as no one knew this part of her history. Here she could take refuge in the bosom of her family and work out what the key, now securely in her bag, was for, and if Sawa could yet be saved. Little did she know that Sawa lay buried under the floor of the secret room in Five Palms House.

After a couple of stops the ferry finally arrived and she disembarked, along with about five other tourists who headed off towards the cluster of buildings on the right, hoping to find a place to stay in the limited bungalow accommodation along the white sandy beach.

Doctor Jah headed off in the opposite direction, and into the jungle via a narrow path. There was no one around, and apart from the tropical birdsong and the odd monkey overhead in the trees, all was quiet. She never used this path at night as there were one or two unsavoury animals in residence, a view shared by others that inhabited Kuantoang Bay, which was by and large isolated from the rest of the island. The daylight was fading so she hurried onwards, steadily descending a small hill.

The jungle thinned to reveal an abandoned palm tree plantation which ended at the sea. The clear ocean ahead concealed a spectacular reef, teeming with fish which lay about a meter below the surface and extended a short way out into the deep blue abyss. Few tourists discovered this natural wonder, so tourism in this undiscovered corner of Thailand was hardly noticeable.

Doctor Jah was walking between the palms when she was spotted by her mother, who immediately sprang to her feet and ran towards her.

***

1999. Getting off Samui

Gerry was taken to the airport after he had hurriedly packed his suitcase. He half expected one of his 'guests' from the secret room to appear and bid him farewell. He barely looked up, and wished he could have done the whole packing thing with his eyes closed, for fear of seeing Nastya. As he emerged from his room, the guards picked up on his unease and wondered what could be wrong. The bully with the vicious temper they knew and feared seemed to be half the man he was, pale and withdrawn.

They watched him get into the chauffeured car and leave, saluting him on the way out of the Five Palms compound. Gerry immediately felt safe and breathed out, taking in the scenery and wondering how on earth he could ever return to the house that hated him. He arrived at the tiny airport, which he considered to be the cutest in the world (which was high praise from a man, who had passed through countless airports in his life).

A small twin-engine plane was waiting on the tarmac, prepared to receive the ten passengers, some of whom had friends bidding them farewell from the thatch-roofed terminal building. Once embarked, the doors were closed for take-off. Gerry glanced over at the well-wisher's waving goodbye and noticed a girl with red hair in the small crowd. "Oh no, not again," said Gerry to himself quickly looking away, feeling his paranoia starting to swell. He bravely looked out of the window again as the plane started to move, returning his gaze back to the girl with the red hair. She caught his eye and smiled, then raised her arm and pointed a finger directly at Gerry who quietly shrieked in horror. This time it was no ordinary redhead. It was definitely Nastya.

***

1999. Can ghosts follow?

Gerry started to sweat profusely after realising what he'd seen. When the seatbelt sign was switched off, the stewardess came over to him and enquired if he was ok. He nodded unconvincingly.

Gerry's journey to London was a living hell, racked in even measure with guilt, doubt, disbelief and horror, an experience which he would never forget. His mind would never be the same again and now for once it was his turn to be on the run, except he didn't know from what!

He arrived back in England and caught a black cab to his penthouse in Ransoms Dock, Battersea. It was a beautiful apartment overlooking a small defunct dock which was tidal, where the muddy, sandy bottom exposed itself at low tide. He could see the beautiful Albert Bridge and the Chelsea embankment from his living room windows and terrace. He could also see Cheyne Court, which he had lied about living at during his exchange with Julian at the pub.

Gerry poured himself a port at the relief of not having seen Nastya on the taxi ride home. He wondered if Nastya wasn't dead after all, or if he had *actually* seen a ghost. Maybe it was just the nerves of having left Five Palms in such a state, combined with fatigue. It was late and he was jet-lagged, but he had to know one way or the other. He rang Five Palms as they were eight hours ahead and just getting into their day.

"Khun Atai?" he asked when the phone was answered.

"Khun Gerry how are you?"

"Fine, fine. Look I need you to do something. Can you dig up the two bodies, the boy and girl. See if they're there?"

Atai paused a moment at this strange request, "But of course they're there. We killed them. We buried them. Why would…"

"Just do it Khun Atai," said Gerry irritated.

"Yes of course, sorry."

"Do it now and report back."

"Yes boss." and Atai ended the call.

Gerry opened the French doors to the balcony and leaned on the wrought iron terrace railings after putting his glass down on the wooden table. His heart began to pound at the prospects of this no-win situation.

Whatever Atai reported back would be bad news. Gerry considered what the worst option would be and concluded a ghost to be the winner. He was hoping that somehow the couple had dug themselves out of their shallow grave and escaped past the guards unseen, despite having been stabbed multiple times. The phone rang an hour later, and the answer wasn't what Gerry expected. It was actually worse.

***

"Boss?"

"Yes."

Atai went quiet.

"Well, what is it? Were they there?"

"It's strange boss. Khun G was…, but Khun Nastya has moved." Gerry could sense Atai's utter confusion.

What? What the fuck are you talking about? They've moved around?"

"Yes."

"But you...we, killed them! I saw the bodies. You saw the bodies. How can they be moving?" Only then did Gerry start to realise the situation - who *had* he seen at the airport?

"I'll call you back. Secure the scene. I hear there is a Detective Gunn prowling around according to P. Bun Ma. Don't tell anybody of this. Understand? It's just you and me."

"Yes boss. Uh, boss?"

"Yes, what is it now?"

"We found some other bones."

"Other bones...look I'm not sure if you're high on Yaba, mushrooms or something, but just tidy up what's there. Pronto. I've got no time for this. Please!"

Atai hung up, annoyed, and went to tidy up the mess.

Gerry sat down by the terrace table. The whole situation, he figured, was like trying to fill up a leaking barrel of water. He looked around suddenly as the living room had no lights on and it was dark, due to the overcast day. He strained his eyes, half expecting to see Nastya in the shadows. He jumped up and turned on the wall lights. His heart was still pounding. He waited to see if Nastya would appear, but she didn't. "This is mad," said Gerry to himself. He considered the strangest thing, *'Do ghosts travel? Do they follow their chosen subject to haunt?'* Immediately he felt these thoughts to be the ramblings of a madman and decided to get drunk. It was his tried and trusted way of ridding himself of jet lag, which he felt was clouding his reasoning. His tried and trusted way to force a catch up on sleep. The downside of a huge hangover was preferable to Gerry to being constantly tired for a week. He put on music and proceeded to undertake the mission.

Gerry woke up at midday the next day. He scoured the room through blurry eyes, and he smiled. Nastya was nowhere to be seen.

He went through his morning ablutions and then made himself a coffee. The Samui problems entered his foggy hungover mind, and he went over what was going on. The most unsavoury problem, ghosts apart, he realised was that the bodies had supposedly moved. To survive such an attack and stabbing would make them superhuman.

Sawa would naturally bring interest from someone, as he learned that missing people always do. And where the hell was Doctor Jah? Did she have the key? He felt like a white king starting a chess match without any other pieces, up against a fully loaded black opposition.

What made things very tricky for Gerry was that he didn't want to go back to Samui for fear of seeing the ghost of Nastya. Gerry thought again about her and wondered whether ghosts could physically harm.

Gerry rang his partner in crime, his long-time friend, Charles Vere. Charles answered surprised, and they arranged to meet at a restaurant in Mayfair.

***

1999. Gunn's conundrum

Gunn drove back to the police station from Big Buddha, wondering what had happened to Doctor Jah.

Unable to wait, he picked up the phone and called Tam. "Tam, hi, any news?"

"On what?" asked Tam with irony.

"Good point," said Gunn, annoyed at the two motorcyclists ahead once again doing the 'foot thing', with each other. He pressed on his horn and stared hard. The two motorcyclists carried on, unaware that Gunn was police.

"Sorry Tam, assholes in front of me, I'm on my way back. I was talking about Jah."

Tam gritted his teeth, "No, sorry boss, I don't know what happened to her. We've got an officer keeping an eye on the surgery."

"Very good. We'll talk about the Sawa witness when I'm back."

"Sure thing." said Tam.

"Oh Tam... no one's reported a missing girl with red hair, have they?"

"Er, no boss."

"Just wondering," said Gunn and put the phone down whilst overtaking the two motorcyclists. He then slowed down in front of them to a snail's pace which aggravated them. He then sped up and slowed down and they followed on his tail. Ahead Gunn saw a large pothole and accelerated again towards it.

The motorcyclists followed, oblivious to what Gunn had seen. Just before the pothole, Gunn swerved to avoid it. The sudden change of direction and speed left the two riders hurtling towards the pothole and they both fell off their bikes after hitting it. Gunn looked in his rear-view mirror and laughed. It was one of his favourite games – it worked every time.

Gunn arrived at the police station, a small, single storey building comprising five rooms, and breezed past the duty officer manning the reception.

"Morning."

"Morning Gunn."

"Tam, there you are. Come and join me, I think I'm going mad."

Tam laughed and joined Gunn at his desk after making a coffee for them both.

"Making people happy eh Tam? You'll go far."

"I know boss, I'll be like you."

Embarrassed at the high praise, Gunn continued, "Let's start with the witness."

"I got his address and he's an established local. He can testify...but to what I don't know. Nor does he apparently. He was both horrified and confused, made it pretty obvious that he was afraid of the people responsible."

"So, he could add nothing more?"

"He did tell us the direction they went after the 'clean up'."

Tam explained the direction to Gunn, which gave him the nagging suspicion it was to Five Palms House, which was very close to the crime scene.

"And Jah? Who was the guy that was shot in the chase?"

"No idea, he's not from around here. He looked Eastern European. His clothes were not from Asia. We checked the labels. His trousers were made in a place called Montenegro, wherever that is."

"Montenegro gangsters in Thailand. Interesting," said Gunn.

"What's going on boss?"

"Something big Tam. Something big," replied Gunn pensively. "Do you know what Tam?

"What?" asked Tam.

"The key. Whoever comes into contact with that key is hunted down. I'm not sure by whom. That's the key, if you'll excuse the pun."

"Oh," replied Tam, although none the wiser.

"The key... is the key," muttered Gunn. "Tam, I think there is a link between a red-haired girl and her boyfriend, who we don't know about yet - but I feel it's coming, and Sawa and of course Doctor Jah." Gunn started to speak his thoughts out loud.

"P. Bun Ma... and a guy called Gerry. P. Bun Ma knows Gerry. The two bodies that bled to death that we never found were right outside Gerry's house. I don't believe they are related because of the time frame but it's a possibility. Do you know what fucks theories up?"

Tam answered no.

"Coincidence. That really fucks things up. But it can be in a good way too. That's called getting a break. Poker or gambling is really calculated coincidence. People put money on calculated coincidence."

Tam looked on bemused at Gunn.

"Sorry Tam."

1999. Time to set sail

Lisa returned to the boat from the hospital.

"How is she?" asked Julian. Lisa's eyes watered as she explained that her mother was now in a coma, and it was now just a matter of 'when' and not 'if'.

A call came through to Lisa and she became inconsolable. The inevitable had happened almost immediately - Lisa's mother had decided to set her daughter free. People on the pontoon watched her collapse on the Lady M's deck, after which Julian took her below.

"I've joined the orphan's club," said Lisa, laughing ironically in between floods of tears. Julian had no idea what to do apart from rendering himself as a useful tea and coffee maker. After about an hour Lisa could once again talk.

***

They gently motored out of Gouvier Marina with Lisa at the helm. Julian had sailed before, but by and large, he was a novice and was later fondly called 'the plank' by Lisa when instigating sailing procedures at sea.

After the funeral, Lisa had decided to sail to Bar Marina in Montenegro, which she knew well from her father's past sailing days. She wanted to get away from Corfu until she calmed down. Julian was very much a 'yes man' during these times and did everything he could to help. Oddly, sex wasn't off the menu and Lisa's orgasms were all-consuming, Julian could feel her enormous release every time. He arrived at the right time in Lisa's life and they both felt this was to be forever.

It was morning, and the wind was perfect for sailing, in just the right direction – NE 20 degrees at about twelve knots. When they rounded the bay, Lisa set the sails and turned the engine off. The boat heeled over by fifteen degrees as the wind caught the sails, pushing the Lady M along at a steady six knots. Julian looked on in awe as Lisa displayed her mastery of the vessel. She popped below and returned a moment later with a drink.

"You'd better have these," and she gave Julian two pills. "They stop the seasickness."

Lisa was reading Julian's mind, and he gleefully took them. Lisa went below once more, and the silence was broken by the opening track off J.J. Cale's album, 5.

"How's that?"

"Perfect," replied Julian as he helmed the boat.

"OK Plank..."

Julian smiled.

"This is a radar..." and Lisa, with a cheeky smile, proceeded to get Julian acquainted with the workings of the yacht. She told him to helm once more and showed him how the autopilot worked. She explained emergency procedures and nautical terms for yacht parts.

"And this is a below job at sea"

"What?" said Julian trying to fathom out this new nautical term whilst trying to helm, "is that something to do with the rudder?"

"Sort of," said Lisa with a very naughty smile, before proceeding to get down on her knees in front of Julian, while pulling his shorts down.

"Oh..." said Julian grinning, "below job, I get it."

***.

"Well, that was interesting," said Julian after Lisa had finished, "is that some sort of rite of passage at sea?"

"Call it what you want, but there are plenty of rites coming your way, and technically, yes, we are on a passage. So, ten out of ten for observation!"

Lisa laughed her unique laugh and Julian felt he was going to really get to like sailing.

They had stayed their course while the wind remained constant for a couple of hours, when Lisa suddenly took the helm, cancelling the autopilot. She loosened the mainsail and swung the boat around, pretty much stopping Lady M in her tracks. "What are you doing?" asked Julian, confused.

Lisa tied off the main sail in a way to resist the front Jenny sail. She locked the helm, so the rudder was fixed at hard to port. The *virtual wind* stopped, and it was incredibly calm. The boat slowly drifted, as if the wind of a few moments ago had vanished by some magic trick. "This is called *'hove to'*," Lisa explained, whilst tying some fenders to *lines* (ropes) and throwing them in the sea.

"It's often used when sailors are exhausted in storms...gives them time to think. Swim and dinner. Agreed?"

"Agreed," said Julian in awe, while Lisa pulled off her bikini and jumped naked into the water after putting the rear step ladder down.

Stunned, Julian followed and jumped into the deep blue sea in the middle of nowhere. Stark naked.

"This is fucking amazing Lisa, amazing!" said Julian before diving under the water to see the hull of Lady M with the deep, deep, bottomless blue sea below.

"She could do with a bath." said Lisa after resurfacing. "Bit of algae on her bum - lets clean it off." She got out and returned, jumping back into the sea with two brushes. She gave one to Julian and proceeded to scrub the algae off the bottom of Lady M. Julian laughed and joined in the underwater fun.

After dinner Lisa asked Julian if he was a night owl or a morning person. Luckily, they were opposites - so Lisa took the morning shift, to relieve Julian at 3am.

"We'll sail under engine power as its easier to react to sudden changes with no sails to deal with...we'll keep the main sail up though; it stops her from yawing. Swaying from side to side that is."

"Ok," said Julian, a little anxious at the thought of sailing alone in the pitch black of night. Darkness fell and Lisa went down below into the rear master cabin, where she could hear the autopilot working. If it stopped functioning, she would hear it immediately, no matter how deep her sleep. Such was Lisa - the seasoned sailor.

Julian adjusted to being on watch and sat fixated for a while on the radar, looking for any white dots that may be heading straight for them. When he calmed down, he sat back and marvelled at the glow of a long-gone sun over the black sea. The sun had gone to find another day in the West. He realised Pink Floyd's song *Time* from *Dark Side of the Moon,* should only be played at sea to get its ultimate impact, but sadly he couldn't turn it up to full volume as Lisa was sleeping directly below.

Julian stood over the GPS at the helm and saw the pre-set destination marked out by Lisa which stopped at Montenegro. He wondered what adventures lay ahead, realising that their lives could be in danger. He questioned why they were pursuing this when they had just discovered such happiness.

Was there a measure of happiness he thought, *'Is happiness able to be scaled? Is it possible to be only slightly happy – you either were or you weren't, surely? Happiness has to be pure, like a clear unpolluted lake. Any pollution meant it's no longer pristine, therefore it burst the bubble of perfection. Can happiness exist without perfection?*

So, what then is the point of this mission? Huge money which would provide security...and that elusive happiness?' He nodded his head, *'money over security equals happiness... until the money runs out.*

So that means time is involved and would determine the volume of happiness. Would you be happy with millions and a day to live? Probably not unless you didn't know. Sooo... time is more important than money - unless you don't know how much time you have. Huh!

So why waste so much of it to get money. The plane would, figuratively speaking, have overshot the runway. I give up.'

"It's amazing what you come up with without any gadgets to distract you," he said out loud in the silence, staring up at the towering full white sail.

***

1999. Why?

Gunn was no longer in a world of fuzz and make-believe. Things were clearer. Seagulls cried overhead and people walked along the beach in the shallow turquoise sea, splashing and laughing in real time. Gunn looked up and saw a palm roof overhead which obscured his view of the blue sky. There were the stairs again beckoning him to descend into the darkness - but this time he felt no need to descend. Then a hand fell lightly upon his shoulder. He jumped and turned around. "Hey, Gunn it's me, G. Remember?"

***

Gunn woke up startled. "G, that's the young man on the beach with the group. The red-haired girl's boyfriend. G." he said out loud, ruffling his long black hair with his hands.

He got up and pulled on some boxer shorts, walked onto the moonlit terrace and continued the conversation with himself. "I never knew his name...did I?" How would I have known it? He must have told me. Why this dream? Why now?"

Gunn got himself together and went to the police station in the morning. For a change there were no mad chases or people going missing, so Gunn had time to collate all the information and try and make some sense of recent events. In this insular island world of his, it felt at times to Gunn that Samui was the crime capital of the world. He sat at his desk and pulled out the photo album he'd found in Sawa's wardrobe. There were about fifty pictures, all developed at local Fuji photo developing outlets. Some were loose and some fixed.

He concentrated on the loose ones first, as he figured they were the ones she looked at the most.

"Weird time to reminisce about your holiday boss," said Tam, looking over Gunn's shoulder.

"Funny Tam, is that my coffee?"

"Sure is."

"Take a seat and check these with me, Sawa's photos from her house" instructed Gunn.

"Ok," said Tam, pulling up a chair.

"I'm looking for a face we may recognise, or places." said Gunn, concentrating on a batch of photos in his hand.

They flicked through them hoping for a prompt, but nothing caught their eye. They looked for messages on the back but there were none. Then Tam came across a faded photo which was older than the rest. He pulled it out. It was of two schoolgirls smiling for the camera and Tam felt this particular photo held a clue. He turned it over, "Bingo!" he shouted.

"What?" said Gunn and took the photo. On the back was Thai writing. 'Sawa and Jah, always together'.

He flipped the photo back over and they both tried to place where it was taken. There were many evenly spaced coconut palms and small bungalows on stilts. There was grass and the sea was behind. "This could be anywhere." said Gunn finally, after scrutinising every detail.

They put the photo to one side and revisited all the others again. Gunn saw one photo that had a boat on it and young Jah and Sawa knee deep in the water next to it by the beach. Gunn took a magnifying glass to it and realised the irony of him holding a magnifying glass - smiling to himself realising that Tam would never get it. He strained his eyes and there was a name on the boat.

"Rasa." said Gunn out loud, attracting Tam's attention. "This is a ferry, and its name is *Rasa*. We need to find ferry companies that have a boat called *Rasa*. I bet it's down south. Can you do that now? If we find this place, I reckon that's where Sawa grew up... with Jah."

Gunn relayed another thought which came into his head. "If Doctor Jah's not dead she's here. I'll bet.

*** *

Mayfair. The Ritz

"Gerry how are you?" asked Charles, already seated at the table. He didn't get up.

"I'm fine Charles. Been a while."

They shook hands over the table as Gerry settled down. "I found a parking meter with money still in it. I think that makes me the happiest when finances are involved."

Charles laughed through his small mouth, making his baby-faced red cheeks glow even more.

"Piling on the weight I see," said Gerry, before Charles could respond.

"Thanks a bloody bunch. Good to see you too."

"Sorry, only teasing."

"I've lost weight you cheeky git...down to 14 stone. Who pushed your perch?"

"I've had a tough ride, you wouldn't believe."

"I can see. You need some oil for the machine...try some of this." The waiter came over and poured a red wine.

"Mmm, nice, Rothschild, right? Which one?"

"Mouton." replied Charles, waiting for Gerry's reaction.

"Bloody what?! That's a thousand pounds a pop. For lunch? What are you on? Oh! you've got news, haven't you?"

"I have and, you're welcome."

"Don't tell me you've been made Chancellor?"

"Even better, old Chancellor Brun has announced he's selling the entire gold reserves of the UK. He got the little letter from Reklem."

"You bloody star! You did it? What did you have on him?"

"Quite a lot. Old Mona got stuck in too. Saucy thing."

"Love her" said Gerry.

"So do a lot of people, it's her job." and they laughed as they clinked their glasses.

"Cheers."

"Cheers." They studied the menu. Gerry looked up and over from the impressive manuscript at Charles. "That stands us in for ten million...each."

"I know." Charles beamed. "Tasting menu?"

"Why not?" The waiter nodded at the simple instruction. For a moment Gerry had forgotten about reality.

"You're joking?"

Gunn left Tam to do his job and went food shopping. Something he despised. He felt the need to cook occasionally to keep his diet on the healthy side, as he figured there was only so much MSG the body could take. All the local eateries used it in abundance. Tourists loved it but the locals, not so much. He picked up a very fine bottle of brandy and when he returned home, poured some into a crystal glass. He sat down, thinking Brandy would be quite an unusual name for a girl when by chance the radio played the song Brandy.

As it finished, the DJ informed him the band was called Looking Glass and that the song was from almost thirty-five years ago... "Huh, I was just using a looking glass today too. What are the chances?" After drinking most of the bottle he headed for the bedroom and looked at the whiteboard on the way. He thought about adding the red-haired girl once more into a separate circle, but instead tumbled into bed.

***

"Hey Tam, any luck?"

Tam had rung and Gunn answered, feeling slightly worse for wear.

"Yes, but I wasn't ringing about that. Had a weird woman come in saying there's a house she passed which has an incredibly bad aura, and that she feels a strong sense of death emanating from within."

"Sure."

"No hear me out, we worked out where this house is. I think it's Five Palms – well, it *is* Five Palms. She described it."

"Here we go again," thought Gunn. "What was her name?" he asked dozily, not ready for the answer.

"Brandy."

Gunn laughed out loud.

* * *

Gunn came into the police station and sat at his desk. Tam joined him and they looked at each other for a moment with a 'where to start' look.

Gunn took the lead. "Ok give me some good news about the boat."

"Well, it's still in service and regularly goes toooo... Kho Ngai, an island off Krabi."

Gunn thought for a moment.

"Brilliant, I think we should go see it. Fancy a break, Tam?"

"You want me to go there?"

"Yup."

"Sure. And look for what?"

"I reckon it's Sawa's or Jah's family home...somewhere on the island. Locals should recognise them. As I remember, it's a sparsely populated, small place. Right?"

"It is."

"Go as a tourist. Get a backpack on, you're young enough. The bird has flown once already." Gunn paused, "unless she's gained the wings of an angel."

"Boss?"

"Dead, Tam. I mean unless she's dead."

"Oh yeah, I see. When do you want me to go?"

"Don't approach her with any force. Slowly, gently. Follow her a little. Go tomorrow... if that's ok with you?"

"Sure, but I'll miss you" said Tam jokingly.

"Get stuffed," said Gunn, realising he'd found not just a prodigy, but a buddy.

"Ok. Now on to the weird stuff. This woman Brandy..."

***

Some questions

"So why the sudden return, did Reklem decide?" asked Charles, tucking into his Michelin starred meal.

"No, it was my call." said Gerry, covering his full mouth and wondering about Charles's strange habit of tucking his serviette into the neck of his shirt in such establishments.

"So why the return?" repeated Charles, "I hear you've knocked some people off."

Gerry spluttered and urgently looked around for eavesdroppers. "Can't you shout that out any louder?"

"All under control. No one's listening."

Gerry spilt some gravy onto his tie and Charles smiled.

"Not such a daft idea after all, eh?" said Charles, grinning at Gerry's mild misfortune. "Come on, spill the beans then."

Gerry was at a crossroads. He needed a confidant. He knew Charles was two-faced, but he was very reassuring and seemed to have retained some morals. From what Gerry saw from his time in Parliament, morals were in short supply, so Charles had *something* going for him. To Gerry, he was corruptible for different reasons. Gerry wanted revenge and Charles wanted money.

Gerry saw that Charles liked to be liked, that was his flaw and why Gerry found him so easy to buy. *Dirty money*, Gerry had said to many, *was like the Titanic - it looked fantastic on top, but it had a big hole below. No matter how many doors you shut...it would still sink.*

Gerry had a few doors which needed shutting as soon as possible. Perhaps Charles could help him close a few.

Gerry took his chance. "I don't want to go back to Samui."

Charles calmly looked up from his meal and finally said, "Why, something wrong old chap?"

Gerry sighed, "A couple of chicanes on my motorway. Sharp ones actually. I think I'm being followed."

"Followed? Followed by who?" asked Charles, his interest piqued.

Gerry realised that if he said a ghost, the show would be over and Reklem or P. Bun Ma would be over in a flash, to work out exactly how mad he was, on a scale of one to ten.

"Well?"

"I'm not sure. Well, a detective. I think"

Charles breathed in and slowly repeated what Gerry had just said, in a more urgent manner. Gerry quickly realised a small hole was starting to form and that he had better stop digging.

"P. Bun Ma informed me of a detective looking around. Asking about the two murders in front of my house in the banana plantation."

"So, what's the urgency? P. Bun Ma owns the police, doesn't he?"

"Yes, to a point, but not all of them are on the payroll, as it were."

"Oh," said Charles in a very 'matter of fact' way. "Well, we'd better have a word."

This was not going in the direction Gerry had intended. Instead of gaining a shoulder to cry on, he'd instigated an investigation into P. Bun Ma.

"There's something you're not telling me I feel," said Charles, "Anything else?"

"No," lied Gerry.

"Listen, I can see you're not all here - let's celebrate another time. £10 million is the beginning I know, but hey!" said Charles reassuringly.

They shook hands outside and parted in separate directions. As he walked to the closest Tube station, Charles played back the lunch conversation on his tape recorder. He didn't notice Gerry across the road, who by chance, had decided to change direction and go by the same route. Gerry saw Charles with the tape recorder and quickly realised he was not the man to help him shut any doors. He said to himself, "Big money, big holes."

***

Brandy

"Well, this woman came in."

"I got that bit," interrupted Gunn with a smile. "I'm not a detective for nothing."

"Funny. Well, she... she had large breasts. No sorry, but she did. Anyway, she said that she felt she had to report feeling a dark presence, an air of deep sorrow and death which shadowed the house. She added, '*a possible murder*'."

"Well, nothing new there, there has been."

"I know and she knew, but she said that there were dead people around, probably in the house."

"Was she nuts? I mean, reporting a 'feeling' to the police?"

"No, she said she realised it sounded strange, but she had a strong intuition for the supernatural. She was about thirty-five, and subtly pretty. Seemed to be all there, said she was from Denmark."

"Sounds like I should meet her socially, anyway... what do you want me to do?"

"She left her number, call her, it can't do any harm."

"No, I guess not. In this weird world."

"Weird?"

"You wouldn't believe." sighed Gunn, still suffering with his hangover.

"Talking of weird, she asked for you by name."

"Ok, pass me the phone."

***

Money

Gerry got a taxi back to his penthouse and figured during the journey, that his 'revenge' link didn't belong in a chain, where all the other links were made up of greed. He was on his own and in too deep to get out. Gerry had known Charles for twenty years on and off, so it was tempting to consider him a friend, but he resisted. He now knew why - his instincts were correct.

He felt crushed by the realisation that there was nowhere or no one he could run to. No soothing, experienced hand to stroke his head during this unusual and unsettling time. Nastya, or whatever it was, had been a mistake he thought with hindsight. He would be on his home turf now if it was not for her, sipping Lagavulin whiskeys at a beach bar. He'd been made homeless, evicted, rendered 'fortunes fool' as in Romeo and Juliet, except he was Romeo without the romance.

He decided to cheer himself up and check his bank account. Sure enough, as agreed, he saw the down payment deposit for the UK's impending gold sale. Five million pounds, with five million to follow after the gold sale conclusion. He started to feel a little better.

***

The Phone Call

"Hi, is that Brandy?" It's Detective Gunn here, how are you?"

Gunn suppressed the obvious question and continued after a second's pause.

"You came into our station looking for me?"

"I did." said Brandy, offering nothing. Brandy liked to play games.

The usually confident Gunn stuttered, "You say there are dead bodies in this house. What brought you there? It's not exactly on the side of a motorway, if you get my meaning."

"I live in two worlds, Detective Gunn. Do you believe in the other side?"

"I'm beginning to wonder. Call me Gunn by the way. It's easier."

"Ok...Gunn," said Brandy in a deliberately evocative way, emphasizing the letter G, which made Gunn move around in his seat at the thought of this 'subtly pretty' Danish girl.

She continued, "I frequent two worlds, ours, and another. Death separates the spirit and the body. I'm sought out by spirits trying to make contact."

"So, you're a medium?" said Gunn, slightly condescendingly.

"I can be, but not exactly. No, I'm different. I can find people in the other world. They can ask me questions."

"Ok. So where do I fit in with this. Where is this leading?"

"Have you noticed some strange things going on in your life recently?" said Brandy, already knowing the answer.

Gunn didn't disappoint and paused. "Well actually, yes. Why?"

"Someone has found you. Perhaps you need to talk?"

"Sure, yes. Where? Er... with you?"

Brandy laughed inwardly, "No Gunn, with the spirit that's found you. But I'll happily meet you as well. Would you like to come to my house?"

"To talk to a spirit. Sure, why not," said Gunn with slight sarcasm, "Are you close?"

"You know the deserted road that crosses the island? I'm sure you do. Well, I'm by the Na Muang waterfalls. The road's been partly washed away so be careful. I'm on the second track, off the main track, leading to the falls."

"Ok," and Gunn put the phone down, still trying to process the strange conversation he'd just had, and how she'd known about the 'odd stuff'.

***

Storm!

Julian thought he saw a flash in the still darkness, making him sit upright in the cockpit. He sat alert in the silence, scanning the horizon but saw nothing more and slowly relaxed again. He felt the sky seemed blacker, but it was hard to differentiate between *blacks*. Then another flash happened. Julian was reluctant to wake Lisa, so he decided to try and see what was going on himself. He noticed the boat had started to heel over a few degrees more, while the wind started to change direction and slightly veer. From his old sailing days, Julian knew this could be prelude to a squall and immediately went below to wake Lisa.

Lisa got up instantly, as if she'd never been asleep. "My father's Musto jacket is in the cupboard there. Put it on. It'll keep you dry and warm. I have to go, sort yourself out and come up. You're going to be useful Plank," and she gave him a smile as she disappeared up the stairs.

When Julian came up, Lisa was at the bow lashing the Jenny sail with a tie, and making sure all was secure.

"Get the main down HALF REEF," shouted Lisa with clarity.

Julian got the winch out and did as he was told. The boat righted slightly and wasn't so overpowered. The wind was getting stronger, and the waves started to get bigger with the lightning flashes becoming more frequent. Lisa stood by the helm and focused on the GPS.

"Let the main out a bit Plank, and then come and see where we are," said Lisa smiling reassuringly. Again, he did as instructed, this time giving Lisa a pinch on the bottom.

"We are not where I wanted to be for a storm," she said loudly. "We are here," and she pointed to the sea between *Lecce* in Italy and *Vlore* in Albania. "The wind, if prolonged, will force us towards the end of the sea trench at Lecce. That won't be nice as the sea will be pushed up its face, creating horrible waves. It goes from 2000m to 50m in under a mile. If anything happens to me, try and stay away from there. Got it?"

"Got it." said Julian, a little worried.

"Ok, I'll go get some Pot Noodles on, this could be a long night."

Julian stood by the helm as the autopilot could still cope with the pressure and watched the squall rapidly advance. He had heard about the Bora winds and how ferocious they could be. He looked anxiously down below, wishing Lisa to hurry up as the yacht was once more heeling hard. There were strong gusts and finally one tripped out the autopilot and the yacht swung violently to port. Julian quickly grabbed the helm and steered her around back to 5 degrees North. Lisa came up. "Having fun?" she enquired calmly, handing Julian a steaming hot Pot Noodle.

The yacht now started to 'nose' into the troughs as the waves became bigger. They watched the wind speed dramatically increase to 38 knots. "Jesus, this is tough!" exclaimed Julian, pushing hard against the wind.

"The sea spray is around 41 knots, a force 9." I'll get some goggles just in case."

The yacht pulled around again and almost threw Julian down, Lisa released the main sail quickly - but remained very much in control.

"IT'S NO GOOD...WE'LL HAVE TO HEAD FOR ITALY." shouted Lisa. "SAIL 340 DEGREES."

She didn't let on to Julian that the waves could get as high as 4m if the yacht reached the end of the underwater trench.

"CAN YOU HOLD HER?"

"YES!" shouted Julian over the blustering wind.

"I'M GOING BELOW TO SECURE THINGS AND GET THE LIFE RAFT OUT." Lisa smiled, "DON'T WORRY, PRECAUTION. THIS SHOULD BE OVER SOON."

Alarmed, but relieved that Lisa was a yacht master and appeared in full control of the situation, Julian helmed hard. The waves piled over the yacht on occasions and water got in below. Lisa came up after about ten minutes.

"WHERE'S THE LIFE RAFT?"

"NOT NECESSARY, THE BAROMETER IS RISING AGAIN. IT'S A SQUALL, NOT A STORM. HOLD FIRM THERE PLANK."

"AYE, AYE!" shouted Julian with a smile of relief.

The wind had started to change direction, and they were allowed to resume their intended course. As the dawn broke, which was late due to the squall, things became calmer, but the seas remained challenging.

The warmth started to seep back into the damp, salty air and they couldn't wait for a shower and cup of tea on terra firma.

"We've passed Tirana, so I reckon we'll be near Bar by dusk." said Lisa looking at the GPS. "It's a shame we were in a minefield though." she said as she looked ahead.

Julian didn't answer at first and finally said "What?"

"Minefield," and Lisa pointed to the boat shape on the GPS which was surrounded by *mine* shaped symbols.

Julian couldn't believe his eyes. They *were* mines. "What the fuck is going on Lisa?"

She gave a telling smile. "It's ok, they're defunct; you *are* jumpy, aren't you?"

"We almost fucking sank back there, so yes."

Lisa laughed again, "It's an ammo dump in the sea from the war. Not dangerous, but it's a good idea to keep going."

The day cleared, and in the very far distance, Lisa saw a tiny cloud illuminated by a setting sun.

"There she is. Black Mountain. Montenegro. She's under that cloud."

"Lisa, the lunch at the Swan," questioned Julian, "How did you know Nick and I would be there? I thought it was a coincidence."

"Your phone was tapped." said Lisa, not flinching as she continued concentrating on the cloud.

"Oh!" said Julian.

"So, you knew you were going to sleep with me?"

Lisa faced Julian and said with a sweet smile, "Yes. Quite an act, wasn't it?"

Rasa

Tam watched the beautiful young men get on the holiday ferry, but sadly for him, most appeared to have girlfriends. He wasn't in a relationship, so he hoped some opportunities may crop up on this break as everybody around was in such a good mood. He considered himself to be a *catch* with his toned shape, dyed blond hair, healthy tan and unusually deep voice, which people usually liked.

He could do with a relationship he thought, but his priority was to focus on finding Doctor Jah. He settled back, and even though he was Thai, and used to Thailand's beauty, he still appreciated all that passed. Tam could understand why everybody around was so happy as he'd heard all about Northern Europe's constant rain and cold.

***

"£100 million?"

"As we're on questions and answers," said Julian letting out the mainsail a little, "you must have been watching me when I met that guy, Gerry."

Lisa sighed, "I was. I was in the next restaurant and was worried as to what the hell he was doing seeing *you*. He's nasty. In fact, I think he's about number 2 or 3 if were ranking the criminal participants."

"How many involved do you think?"

"Hundreds, if not thousands."

"Fuck me... that's massive."

"It is. I've seen it escalate, seen people try and get out, only to be let's say, silenced." Lisa raised her eyebrows.

"So, what exactly is your angle in all this?"

"Money."

"That's honest."

"At first, I thought I could blackmail the criminal perpetrators, which in my view would be an ethical thing to do, but then I realised how big this was. I could have - but ran the risk of still being taken out at any time. That's when I sought security from a trusted member of the government, so I found Timmingham."

"Who's he?"

"I'll explain another day. I'm still not sure. But I struck a deal to save the UK's and the West's gold. I would take one percent, or a hundred million. They offered a hundred million. That's why I'm here. Ta daa! I had to involve you because, by accident, you ended up on their hit list."

"Why don't they just ask you to divulge your information...for free. The Treason act or something like that?"

"Half the cabinet are in on it. It's hard to tell who's in, or out. Blackmail is the main driver. Someone owns them all. And that's what we're onto. I'm afraid you're in, like it or not."

"A hundred million?"

"A hundred million." repeated Lisa, reassuring herself. "The West's gold reserves add up to a lot, as you can imagine. So, it's a price worth paying in their eyes. Plus, immunity and a safe location after the shit hits the fan. I, now we – disappear!"

"So, I'm in on the payroll?"

"You're with me darling, so yes. Besides, it'll be fun!" Lisa looked at Julian and widened her eyes.

"Beats working in a kebab shop I guess, so great! But sorry, I wouldn't trust anyone to honour £100 million."

"No choice sweetie, I already have some of it. Not just a pretty face you know. I have a man who's syphoned off an amount without them noticing. After all, it's how they got it in the first place. No one noticed. It's hard to count such a mass of gold every day."

"May I ask where it is?"

"Europe's gold?... in a disused submarine silo."

"Let me guess, Montenegro?"

"Ooooh, someone's a live wire today. Yes." said Lisa with mock sarcasm. Land ahoy!"

"If we live" said Julian, to see Lisa's reaction to the statement. Chillingly, she confirmed his fears, repeating his question staring ahead, "Yes, if we live..."

Cristal, Brandy

Gunn turned down an inconspicuous road off his 'favourite' coastal drive, about five minutes before the Bo Phut T-junction. After a short drive, the shanty sprawl of houses diminished and gradually gave way to some untended plantations - and then wild jungle. The road started to rise suddenly, and very steeply, up the mountainside. There were no cars, as only locals knew of this short cut across the island, and even they seldom used it, as it was fairly treacherous and renowned for collapse.

After about half an hour he found the road leading to the waterfalls, and as instructed took the second turning down a gravel track through the jungle for about two minutes, until he saw Brandy's house. It was a stilted, rambling bungalow and Gunn admired its unusual architecture.

He stopped the car, got out and surveyed the area. "Nice, isn't it?" said a voice. Brandy was standing in the shadows of a tall bush, near the house.

Gunn looked around and stared briefly at her, "Yes unusual. It looks colonial."

"That it is" said Brandy and approached Gunn to shake his hand.

"Do you know me from somewhere?" asked Gunn, wondering about her familiarity.

"No, and you're staring."

Gunn realised what he was doing and looked up quickly. Before he could answer, Brandy said, "Everybody does, I don't mind. If I were a man, I would too probably."

Gunn for once was totally lost for words after not realising that he was indeed glancing at Brandy's breasts. Tam had warned him, even though Tam was gay.

"Coffee?" said Brandy, as if nothing had happened.

"Anything, I mean yes. Look, I'm sorry if I was being inappropriate, I'm..."

"I told you, everybody does. It's natural, isn't it? Come" and Brandy led him into the house and through to the living room which had views of the falls.

"That's pretty special," said Gunn, and the conversation, mercifully for him, moved away from Brandy's breasts.

"You should see it during monsoon. Oh, here's my sister Cristal."

Cristal came into the room and said, "Hi."

She was equally as attractive as Brandy, and Gunn thought it was pretty risky for both of them to be living alone, in such a remote place.

"Well, I'm here to follow up your assertion that there's a house which you think has been the scene of a murder."

"Yes. I felt you should know. Someone from my *other world* is, let's say, very angry. She said to contact you and told me your name. She's been watching you and mentioned something about circles. Does that mean anything to you?"

Gunn paused, "Well, actually it does and would answer a question."

"Good, glad I could help there. There is confusion for me too and maybe you could assist?"

"Fire away."

"I thought that's what guns did, don't want to steal your thunder," and both girls laughed as Cristal brought in the coffees.

"Very funny, that's a new one to me, any others?"

"Ok. Is your partner at the station called Rick O' Shea?" said Cristal.

Gunn smiled at his two beautiful hosts, who were clearly enjoying pulling his leg, and wondered if they'd had something before he arrived.

"It's a strange one," continued Brandy. "You see, people who talk to me are normally dead, but I'm not sure if this one *is*. She's operating in both spheres. She's in both *our* world, and the other one - at the same time. So, I don't understand how she can communicate with me. This is why I decided to visit."

"It's a new dimension, I'll give you that." said Gunn. "No chapter in my training manual covers this. I think I know what you're talking about, but don't understand it in the slightest. You did, however send a tingle down my spine when you mentioned circles though. To know of that, means in my mind, that I must take you seriously. And I don't mean to sound condescending, in the least, with that last remark."

Gunn sipped his coffee, trying desperately not to look at Brandy's anatomy which was compressed into tailored, deliberately tight-fitting garments. Gunn was drawn to a certain attractive quality about her, which was emphasised by her spirituality. He continued, "The house you mentioned appears to match a private residence called Five Palms House. It's owned by an English MP called Gerry Absalom. It will be very hard to obtain permission to search that house, unless you have something from 'this world', to help us.

"What about the two murders before?" asked Cristal, who once again silenced Gunn. With nothing to lose, he replied openly,

"Not related, and we did look around then, but faced great resistance. No obstruction as such, but we had limited access. Do you have anything more?"

"No. Not really."

"So, who is this *contact*?" asked Gunn.

"It's a girl. She doesn't say much, but I can feel her wrath. She doesn't reveal herself to me, which makes me question whether she's alive or dead. One noticeable thing though, she has red hair."

"No shit," said Gunn, as though half expecting this.

"You know her?" asked Brandy, who for once during their brief interaction, seemed unusually uninformed.

"She's on my radar shall we say. A friend of hers called Lisa has been looking for her and her boyfriend G. The other day actually... I got a tip off."

"Do you know G?"

"You're not going to believe this – but he came up in a dream I had, where he mentioned his name to me. It's been a recurring dream that finally became clear...oddly enough on the day you came into the police station." Gunn sat back on the sofa.

"Someone's been trying to reach you?" pondered Brandy, "G. I wonder if *he's* dead? He's not found me, so I'm not sure." said Brandy.

"Ladies, this is all too weird for me, so unless we have something concrete, I can't force a search. I must go as other stuff calls, you know."

"I do," said Brandy, "by the way, are you married? Girlfriend? Boyfriend?"

Gunn shook his head, "No, and I'm not gay, why? Anybody in the other world interested?"

"No... just someone in this world," and Brandy beamed at Gunn whilst sipping her coffee.

Gunn said goodbye to the sisters, got into his car and drove back down the dirt track. When he was out of sight, he looked in the rear-view mirror and gave himself the biggest smile.

***

Who were the other skeletons?

Gerry's mind was a mess. He couldn't work out why Charles had recorded their lunch meeting. Surely, he thought, he's not plotting against me? Gerry had known Charles for a long time, and they had acquired a few secrets along the way which were best kept between them, as they could have caused Charles some rather serious marital damage. *Is that what relationship end games are about? Spilling the beans? Who could come up with the most damaging occurrences with which to accuse the other?* Gerry decided that if this were not true, *lawyers wouldn't have 80% of their clients. At least my violence is 'honest', and of the day, not some event stored up as ammunition, to be used another time to create havoc.* He wondered if it were time for some honesty in the group. Whatever his decision, he would wait for the other £5 million to come into his account. Chancellor Brun was days away from off-loading most of the UK's gold reserves.

There was still no sign of Nastya, so Gerry figured that problem was far away, although he did wonder who the other bones belonged to. He smiled ironically at the thought that they weren't anything to do with him and that some previous development had occurred at the house before he'd arrived on the scene.

Despite this brief bemusement, it raised the serious question as to who exactly they belonged to?

Just as he was about to embark on this journey of thought, Khun Atai rang.

"Atai," said Gerry with trepidation, "What's going on?"

"Well Khun Gerry, the other bones…"

"I was just thinking about that, whose are they?"

"I don't know. There are about four bodies, skulls."

Gerry went silent for a moment, working out that the newly discovered 'tenants' equated to nine expired residents under the house. That would make international news. Especially as Gerry was a politician. *'Establishment British politicians murder house,' 'How many more?'* The imaginary headlines crushed Gerry's mind.

"They're nothing to do with me," replied Gerry defensively, as if it made any difference.

"Sure officer, these are mine but the others? I've got no idea."

"That's ok then sir, quite a relief actually. We thought for a brief moment that you may have exceeded your murder quota for the year," said the imaginary policeman dressed in a Victorian-era uniform.

"It must have been the last owner," said Atai, breaking the silence and trying to be helpful.

"Doesn't help me much. But can you find out about them please. And thank you." Atai was taken aback by Gerry's politeness, and figured something was up with Gerry, who he was beginning to resent.

Gerry put the phone down and decided it was time to tie up a few loose ends. He rang Charles.

"Hi Gerry."

"Charles, why did you record our conversation?", said Gerry, getting straight to the point.

"What?" Charles stalled, wondering how Gerry knew of the recording.

"What recording?" asked Charles again, briefly thinking if there was another recording which he didn't know about.

"Our lunch mate."

"You think I recorded our lunch? I couldn't afford the film crew. What are you on about?" said Charles, slightly agitated.

"I saw you listening to a recorder. You were walking to the tube... after our lunch."

"Aaah! I was listening to my memos of things to do, stupid. I record stuff. Reminders, you know? I have no interest in stealing the chef's recipes. They would litigate."

"Really?" said Gerry, wanting to believe Charles.

"Yes really, what the fuck's up with you old buddy? You seemed really weird at our little 'celebration'".

"Sorry. There's been a lot going on. Just a misunderstanding is all. Listen, can I buy you a drink? I need to get a few things out there."

"Sure, when? Sounds urgent." said Charles, pretending to calm down.

"It is, I suppose. Tomorrow?" said Gerry, trying to sound like his old self.

"Sure, the Scarsdale Pub, Kensington?"

"Good call. see you then. Eight?"

"Eight." and Gerry hung up, relieved.

***

Escape

Tam got off at the beach, second stop after the jetty at Koh Ngai. The tourists piled off first, and Tam headed for a reception at some nearby holiday bungalows. The receptionist was arguing over a tin of 'Cockroach Killer', as it transpired from the discussion that there was only one on the island, and there was no way she was going to let it go. The tourist walked out in disbelief and Tam watched the receptionist hide the repellent under the counter.

Being careful not to act as too much of a policeman, Tam pulled out the photo and asked the receptionist in Thai if she recognised the place where Doctor Jah and Sawa were sitting. She did and told him it was across the other side if the island. He then asked if she recognised the girls, which she did not, so he asked if she could ask if any of her colleagues did. She obligingly went to the back office to check.

An older lady came back out with the receptionist, holding the photo.

"Yes, I know these girls. This one is now a doctor," she said proudly pointing at the girl on the left. "Doctor Jah. She's working on Samui."

"Can you tell me anything about her or her family?"

"Why don't you ask them? They still live here, and Doctor Jah is back visiting."

"Really?" said Tam. I'll do that, thank you. I'll go now if you could tell me how to find them. By the way do you have any rooms?"

"For you, yes. A friend of Doctor Jah is a friend of mine. You are a friend, right?"

"Sort of. I'm here to look after some matters. I'm a friend."

"Oh," said the lady, looking slightly suspicious. "Here you are, Bungalow 2, over there."

"Thank you."

Tam's wooden bungalow overlooked paradise on an epic scale. Sea, islands, beach and tranquillity without a road or car in sight. He rang Gunn.

"At last, a break. Good job Tam," said Gunn still in a buoyant mood after Brandy's earlier remarks.

"I can't arrest her; she's done nothing wrong. What should I do?"

"Ask her point-blank about the key. Explain that she is in real danger. Ask if she would return to Samui with you."

"I guess with information like that she will."

"Off you go then, chop-chop."

"I'll let you know."

"Oh, Tam..."

"Yes?"

"Don't lose her. This is a big deal. Get the key, and fish will come for the bait."

"Understood boss."

After breakfast the next day, Tam went to check out the bay across the other side of the island. After a short hike up and over the tree-clad hill in the middle of the island, he emerged from the jungle into a serene landscape which hadn't changed for hundreds of years. Wisps of thin white smoke rose from in between the stilted wooden huts of the small village. Tam wondered if the inhabitants had even heard of the Second World War!

There was one recent addition in the form of a café made of bamboo and coconut wood, a place for curious tourists who chose to explore this side of the island to refresh themselves. Tam checked the photo of Doctor Jah once more before making his way to the café. His bleached blond hair stuck out a mile and a couple of locals stared at him unashamedly, thinking that yet another Thai had succumbed to decadent, Western culture.

He sat down and ordered a coffee, then looked around peacefully, taking in the silence. The sea beyond the palm trees was in view and still. Exotic birdsong broke the tranquillity overhead and he watched the odd local pass by. Some tourists broke through the wall of jungle behind him and ran excitedly towards the sea, shouting happily at each other. Tam broke a smile, as they took off their sweaty shirts and jumped into the shallow sea.

"There's a reef here!" said one in amazement, and the others proceeded cautiously after their leader.

Tam was wondering about his next steps when Doctor Jah suddenly appeared on the wooden terrace and sat down on a nearby bench. She gave him a polite smile and he smiled back. There was no phone signal here, so people tended to sway back to their natural instincts and became more sociable. The owner and Doctor Jah started to talk and tried to include Tam, who joined the conversation reluctantly for fear of blowing his cover.

"Are you on holiday?" asked Doctor Jah in Thai.

"Sort of, how about you?"

"Also sort of." Doctor Jah gave another small smile and sipped her coffee. The owner joined in with some small talk and then left for her kitchen.

Tam decided to make a move as things were moving quickly, and it would be no surprise to him if a Montenegrin turned up wielding a gun.

"You don't look like you live here, are you from elsewhere?" asked Tam slightly awkwardly.

"Yes." said Doctor Jah hesitantly, caught unaware by the probing question, as she too was expecting trouble.

"Where do you live?" asked Tam, knowing the answer.

"Why?" asked Doctor Jah.

"Just wondered." and Tam breathed in, "Look, I'm a policeman and you're in danger."

Doctor Jah almost spat out her coffee and sat up straight on the bench. Instinctively she looked for an escape route whilst thinking of an answer.

"Please be calm, I can prove who I am - and you can trust me, but you *are* in danger." Tam didn't move and looked deeply into Doctor Jah's soul.

The impasse lasted a short moment as both unwittingly waited to see who was going to move first.

"Prove it!" said Doctor Jah assertively.

"I will. We just need to make a phone call to my station on Samui to prove who I am."

With this revelation, Doctor Jah relaxed.

"You can find the phone number of Nathon police station and ask to speak to a Detective Gunn. He can explain the situation and describe me, which I hope will be complimentary," and Tam grinned realising that he was gaining her trust.

"Ok." said Doctor Jah, clearly relieved.

A land line was available in the café as the internet had not yet made it to this corner of the world. She found the phone number and dialled nervously, speaking to the reception once the line was picked up. Silence followed as she waited to be put through to a surprised Gunn.

After a brief enquiry and apparent confirmation, Doctor Jah passed the phone to Tam. Tam took some instructions and put the phone down.

"Do you have the key?" asked Tam, getting straight to the point.

"No," said Doctor Jah flatly.

"Oh, so you do know about '*a*', key?"

Doctor Jah was stumped. She had failed at the first attempt to conceal her knowledge.

"Look Doctor Jah, you are in great danger, we believe your life could be on the line. You saw what happened at your surgery. That man is dead. Shot by his own people. You need protection. My biggest concern is Nurse Sawa. Do you know where she is?"

There was a lot of information for Doctor Jah to digest, and she stalled.

"Liars always have to think before they give an answer" said Tam unprompted.

Doctor Jah said she'd not heard from Sawa and explained tearfully about how they grew up together on the island.

"She's probably hiding somewhere like you," said Tam unconvincingly, trying to stop Doctor Jah's tears. "We need to get you to safety. We believe that whoever is hunting you will back off, if they see you with us."

Doctor Jah considered the offer for a moment before nodding in agreement.

"We don't want to let whoever they are, know that your mother is here. You must tell her a story, so she knows nothing. You understand? We must protect her. We will have someone watch the village for a while until we understand things better. Now I'll give you a while to do what you need to do."

"Ok," said Doctor Jah.

"And don't forget the key!"

Doctor Jah nodded and left.

Tam rang Gunn and explained the situation.

"Now we have our bait," said Gunn, "Prepare for sharks."

Doctor Jah came out from the family house and gave her mother a hug. While it looked like she suspected nothing, she still stared at Tam, who nodded back in acknowledgement.

"Ok, let's go." said Doctor Jah.

"What did you tell her?"

"That someone had tried to rob the surgery."

"Good call," said Tam, "and the key?"

"Here. What the hell is this thing anyway?"

"Honestly?" said Tam, "I've got no idea... personally I think it's evil and the sooner I can give it to the relevant authorities, the better." Tam took Doctor Jah's bag, and they proceeded along the hilly, dusty path that led through the still jungle in concentrated silence. After about ten minutes they stopped.

"Did you hear that?" said Doctor Jah, looking behind her.

***

Time for *that* question?

Gunn was in a quandary. The key was not for him to keep and technically he should return it to its owner, should they be known. He suspected it to belong to Gerry from the Five Palms House, but there was nothing to prove this theory. He knew Five Palms held a lot of secrets behind its doors, to the point where even self-proclaimed mediums were telling him to explore there. 'Brandy said she had a feeling something's up, can we come in and turn the place over?' didn't seem to be a good reason, but then Gunn had an idea.

P. Bun Ma, Gunn knew, had influence over many of the police in the area, although he wasn't entirely sure *who* was under his wing. Gunn knew Gerry had some sort of connection to P. Bun Ma and he was basically warded off from approaching him. So what if, Gunn pondered, he turned up with the key at Five Palms, asking if belonged to Gerry? He could gain entry and possibly look around, whilst a fellow officer distracted the occupants of the house.

The key would not be the original – because... Gunn tried to think of an answer. He would have to do this without P. Bun Ma's knowledge, and if caught he would simply say that he was there to pass on a key which he believed belonged to Gerry. If P. Bun Ma were to realise that he was directly approaching Gerry, then... suddenly it occurred to Gunn. Now he was a target!

Gunn realised that of all the people, *he* was the one that should watch out. This 'seeing the wood for the trees', moment hit Gunn hard as he knew that when one person works something out, others have too. For all he knew, bullets with his name on them were being loaded while he was having this very thought.

Gunn then went to another level and considered dropping the case, but decided that because he was so far in, this was no longer an option. Whatever was going on had serious money behind it and involved Eastern European men. Gerry's potential involvement truly made it international. Like waking up and deciding if one should go for a pee in the middle of the night or just wait, putting off the decision to visit Five Palms would only prolong things - and potentially make things worse. It was time to revisit his whiteboard.

***

No internet. No reception. What century is this?

"It sounded like a twig breaking." said Tam to Doctor Jah. They remained still, not daring to move, straining their hearing to detect any sound. Their eyes focused watching for movement, but still nothing!

Then the sound of rustling leaves could once again be heard, except this time it was from a different location.

Silence followed once more.

"Run now!" whispered Tam urgently to Doctor Jah. "Go Now. I'm right behind you."

Doctor Jah obeyed, and they ran as fast as they could through the jungle and then stopped, out of breath after five minutes. Suddenly Doctor Jah stepped off the path and surreptitiously disappeared into a concealed opening in the overhanging foliage. Tam followed instinctively, knowing what Doctor Jah was up to, realising she knew this jungle like the back of her hand. They ended up at a hidden cave in which they cowered.

"There's another way out, so we're not trapped," whispered Doctor Jah. Tam nodded, relieved at the potential plan 'b', and they remained silent.

"Could be tourists?" guessed Tam, still a little breathless.

"Hmmm." said Doctor Jah unconvinced. Tam understood this was her territory now, and experience had taught her to recognise every sound - from monkeys to birds, and most of all, people. All remained calm until they heard in the distance something pass them on the trail to the main beach. They did nothing. Then all was calm once more.

"We have to go back to check on my mother. They may have seen us with her, if there actually is a 'they'."

Tam agreed, as he didn't want a hostage situation, so they moved towards the village after waiting fifteen minutes. Doctor Jah, as a precaution, took them a different way back to her house. When they emerged from the jungle, they were horrified to see two men sitting at the café, who were clearly not locals or tourists and didn't look very friendly.

"I bet they're Montenegrin." said Tam under his breath.

"What?" asked Doctor Jah.

Tam didn't answer and remained focused on the two big men, wondering if they knew about Doctor Jah's mother. Doctor Jah was thinking the same thing. Tam was frustrated that he couldn't communicate or ask for backup as without technology, they were isolated hunted animals, alone, on a small island. They would have to come out at some point, so they needed to do something. One of the men faced their way without seeing them. Tam recognised him from the ferry.

"Fuck!" said Tam quietly, acknowledging the fact that he'd been followed. He wondered if there was a mole in the police station and realised it could be anybody. He then had a wild thought. Gunn?

"They don't know it's your mother's place. They would have taken her by now. I wonder if they know what you look like?" said Tam breaking away from his crazy mental ramblings. Doctor Jah had no answer.

"I think your mother's safe. We should leave here so they don't put two and two together. Is there any other way off this island?"

Doctor Jah's eyes lit up, "Yes, a fisherman. Come."

They slid back into the bushes and Doctor Jah went the opposite way from the village and along the waterfront. After about five minutes a small wooden jetty could be seen, and in the distance a man fishing on a boat. Doctor Jah shouted.

The man looked up and rowed towards them, instantly recognising Doctor Jah. After the formalities were over, in which Tam played no part whatsoever, the man said he could take them, unseen, to *Koh Kradan*. The shallow waters that lapped up on the paradise beach were so clear that only wave motion gave away that the sea was there at *all*.

"How far is it to Kradan?" asked Tam, unconvinced.

"About 20 kilometres," said the fisherman.

"We'll be rowing for about four weeks if the tide's against us." smirked Tam sarcastically.

"I have engine." and the man pointed to a shed where the engine was housed.

Doctor Jah gave a little sarcastic sideways smile at Tam.

They got into the boat with the sun falling low in the sky and headed towards *Koh Wean*, a magnificent towering limestone island protected by sheer cliffs allowing, for once, for nature to have its own way. Immediately after they passed this feature, the silhouette of Koh Kradan came into view. The three Thais couldn't help but appreciate the spectacular nature all around them. Once they finally arrived at the island, they headed for a beach which had an isolated tourist establishment called *The Sand Bar,* easily spotted from the sea by its tables dotted around on the sand.

"I know the owner," said Doctor Jah after the relatively communication-free journey. "I can phone back to where you were staying and get your things."

"Thank you. I can get us dinner on the house courtesy of Nathon police station, but I need to call Gunn, ASAP."

"I'll need to call my mum to see if she's ok, and don't worry, I won't let on." replied Doctor Jah.

The old fisherman wished to go home despite the offer to stay, so they bid him a safe journey and he left despite the darkness.

"I hope I don't have to that again," said Tam, and Jah nodded.

***

The whiteboard

Gunn looked at the information on his whiteboard for the last time, then wiped it clean, feeling that his house was no longer safe. He checked outside the window at the front and saw no one. He relaxed and phoned Brandy.

"Hello?"

"Hi, it's me," said Gunn, "my other number - for you. It's safe."

"I know lover, you've got some problems."

"What problems?" asked Gunn, knowing she knew.

"You have decisions to make, don't you?"

"What should I do?" asked Gunn, playing along.

"There's someone putting a block on you, your wings are tied."

Gunn frowned and said nothing, hoping she wasn't referring to P. Bun Ma.

Brandy was a little disappointed that he didn't believe her instincts and intuition, but experience taught her not to expect it.

"You've realised that you are the problem for somebody, and I see it's somebody in a faraway land. I've seen a big lake. Water… and a mountain. Do you know of such a person or place?"

"No. Look I miss you; can I see you?"

"Changing the subject won't help, but I have to say you were a very naughty boy sneaking back the other day. That could have got us into a lot of trouble."

"Oh!"

"But you were worth it. It was a nice, unexpected surprise. Do you do that often?"

"What kind of question is that? "protested Gunn playfully.

"Don't know, but sis realised you were the real deal PDQ and made lame excuses to vacate. Bless her. So yes, I want to see you."

"So can I?"

"No!"

"Terrific, Why?" Gunn replied in a slightly less confident tone.

"Circumstances, My sources tell me not yet, if we want to stay alive, that is. A red-haired girl is telling me that Five Palms is where we need to go… it's why we met. She never told me about you though. She's playing with me a little, but in a friendly way. She's still angry though."

"I think I have an idea what you're saying. If I go there, can you see what will happen?"

"No."

Gunn sat back in his chair and drummed his fingers on his desk, "Ok, I hear you. I'll call you later. Ok?"

"I miss you."

"Miss you too."

Gunn put the phone down and smiled. "She loves me." he said out loud to himself and watched the sea. He broke off his feeling of euphoria when he heard something drop in his office. He got his gun from his bedside drawer and cautiously approached the office seeing that the door was ajar.

Gunn cocked the trigger of his gun and lowered himself quietly to the floor. He always did this in these types of situations, and he could never understand why people ran upright into possible armed situations, without knowing what they were about to face. He pushed the door wide open, threw some coins into the room as a noise distraction and rolled past the threshold. He quickly assessed his position, pointing his gun in front of him but saw no one.

There was nothing but silence. He was sweating, something he rarely did, and saw a black marker pen on the floor – beneath the white board. His eyes slowly looked up at the board and saw a childishly written number '5' on the top right corner. He didn't bother to look around as he knew this was no ordinary situation. Whatever wrote the number on the board was not of this Earth.

***

Gunn was now at the stage where he expected the unexpected, but the expected was nowhere to be seen. He thought back to how on earth he had gotten into such a situation. Two phone calls about a key, he remembered, which now prompted him to ring Tam and find out what was going on.

"Boss, I like it here" said Tam, grateful to be connected again.

"I'm sure. When you get back to the station do not mention Jah. Tell everybody you had a personal issue and took time out. Say you told me, and I'll say I forgot to mention it. I'm trusting you on this."

"Appreciate your trust. I won't let you down. FYI, it's worth mentioning that Jah's awfully confused."

"I'll call her now. Be careful Tam, we have enemies."

"I figured. Again, you can count on me."

And with that, just as Tam put the phone down, 'You Can Count on Me' by Superheart played on the radio. Gunn raised his eyebrows at yet another coincidence, it was one of his favourite songs.

Gunn went back to the office when the song had finished, and '5', was still on the board. He wiped it off.

***

Trouble in Paradise

It had been brought to P. Bun Ma's attention that a Doctor Jah was now involved - and missing. He was displeased. The elusive key was causing havoc, and he felt the situation was now going to have to involve him directly. He couldn't fathom out why, with literally all the funds in the world at their disposal, a simple key with *peasants* involved, couldn't be found.

Gunn had also entered the frame, which really was a problem as Gunn knew of the unscrupulous behaviour that went on with him defrauding the government in a coastal land acquisition transaction.

Gunn had accidentally walked into the proceedings via P. Bun Ma's lawyer during a murder inquiry — the lawyer was involved in both cases simultaneously. This lawyer couldn't hold his drink and had a big mouth, which had probably cost him his life as he was nowhere to be found. Confidentiality was clearly not his forte. Gunn was therefore a loose cannon in P. Bun Ma's eyes.

P. Bun Ma never brought up the subject in case Gunn knew nothing but presumed he did. Gunn therefore received superstar treatment from the mafia, even though he'd never asked for it. It was figured that the more Gunn was bribed, the less he'd be able to reveal the truth, as he was technically corrupted by accepting the favours. This point was now partially true, but P. Bun Ma didn't like loose ends, of which there were now many.

With the recent events of Gerry leaving the island, the key, Sawa, Doctor Jah and foreign agents being shot, P. Bun Ma saw that the situation was a tinderbox. It was time to act.

***

"Tam, how is Doctor Jah doing?" said Gunn over the phone. "Not really sure what to do with her, this is getting tricky. Did you mention to anyone where you were going? Does anyone know about her?"

"Of course, we needed backup remember? So, I guess everyone knows. On top of that, the dead foreign agents. Thinking about it - who *doesn't* know?" replied Tam.

Gunn thought for a second. "Yes, yes, sorry being stupid. Who knows about the key though?"

"That's a good point. No one's really interested in Doctor Jah, so just you and me I guess."

"And Doctor Smith."

"Yes."

"And Sawa."

"Yes."

"And the man at Five Palms...probably."

Tam shook his head, "I guess."

"Do you know P. Bun Ma? Has he ever approached you?"

Tam was taken aback by this question and paused for a moment as he thought how to reply.

"Yes" he said simply.

"And?"

Tam sighed, "Well he told me to keep him informed of any irregularities."

"Irregularities? That's a strange one. You know he's quite influential in the department, don't you?" pressed Gunn.

"I do... and I have to tell you this. After the recent events, I'm a bit worried. It's been mentioned that I've stepped out of line by head office over the shooting."

"Really."

"And they asked me about you."

"Anything else?"

"My flat was upgraded for no reason, and I got a pay rise without asking."

"I see," said Gunn. "What's your take on this?"

"Looks like I'm being bought."

Gunn raised his eyebrows, "Yeah, sure looks that way." Gunn thought for a moment in silence.

"So, what are you going to do. You don't need me?"

"I know. I'm at a crossroads."

"Ok Tam, here goes."

Gunn went onto explain about his ideas on the key and its value. He explained about Lisa and Julian. He divulged that there was big money involved and then asked Tam if he would join him.

"I believe we're talking millions," concluded Gunn.

Tam momentarily held the phone away from his ear and then said, "Looks like money buys everything. Count me in."

Gunn breathed out.

The Scarsdale

Gerry hurried down to the street to grab a taxi for the meeting with Charles. The traffic was gridlocked and the cab ground to a halt on the Albert Bridge, barely two minutes away from Gerry's flat.

As he looked out the cab window, Gerry's troubled mind wandered and wondered about how he'd ended up in such a bad place. He was a human who couldn't seem to get along with other humans.

'Why were they so complex, why is everything they do so confrontational? 'Countries always at war, people constantly fighting each other. Boxers fighting, couples fighting, tribes fighting, religions fighting, lawyers fighting - everything he thought was about competing or fighting. His mind continued down this depressing track,

'Runners compete, teams in games compete, kids in schools compete, siblings compete... impressing, competing or fighting is all we do. Even the sex act is aggressive at the end with the screaming and shouting.'

'Why? For money? To impress a potential mate, or to keep a mate? ... is this why I am where I am? The system is rotten, politicians and so called 'leaders' thrive on this. Divide and conquer. They are the masters as they, and now I, have the power to print money. I've got where I am to impress? Perhaps I can change things. Now there's a thought. Vote for me. Killer Gerry. I'll change things for the better or I'll bury you under my house'.

His thoughts were broken by a cyclist swearing at the taxi driver, who suddenly pushed forward to keep up with the moving cars ahead of them. Gerry then smiled at his last thought and remembered a motto passed around Chambers which read, *'The bankers will ensure we stay in debt. The pharma companies will ensure we stay sick. The arms manufacturers will ensure we keep going to war. The media will ensure we are prevented from knowing the truth. The government will ensure all of this is done legally'.*

He got out of the cab at Edwards Square and there stood the *Scarsdale* pub. Charles, as usual, was early and waved at him from his spot on a bench by a tree in the front garden.

"Gerry. Would you mind speaking into this pen?" and Charles blew into it and tapped it as if it were a microphone.

"Very funny, but welcome. I could do with a laugh."

"Clearly. I got you a pint in anticipation."

"You star, cheers," and Gerry downed half of it, as if his life depended on it."

"Crikey. You never seen one of those before?" said Charles, feigning admiration.

"Not for a few hours, no!" joked Gerry, with a smile which Charles still found unnerving. Charles imagined Gerry's victims seeing the same sinister facial contortion.

Charles refocused.

"You remind me of a mathematician who's afraid of negative numbers,"

"Go on," said Gerry.

"You'll stop at *nothing* to avoid them." continued Charles in a dead pan voice looking at the square.

Gerry sniggered, "Very droll."

"The deal is done. Brun sold the gold. Perhaps he believed in 'fool's gold'."

"What are you on?" said Gerry looking up from his pint.

"I'm happy, and rich. We just creamed the other five million. Italy's about to cough up soon as well. That means another ten!"

"Shit, when did that happen?"

"Yesterday. You all here old chum?" Charles put his hand on Gerry's shoulder. "Brun has sold the UK's gold at bottom dollar. Of course, we stole the rest, but no one's looking."

"Reklem's got it right? Or P. Panya?" asked Gerry, referring to P. Bun Ma's partner.

"One of them, but why care? We've been paid. Cheers!"

Gerry raised his glass, "Cheers."

The evening went on for a few hours and the pair got a little drunk as the pub filled up with people in a similar state.

"Old days."

"Old days," replied Charles and they loudly knocked their glasses together. Charles breathed out and shouted above the noise, "There's something you should know old boy."

Gerry laughed, "What?"

"I'm serious," said Charles, stiffening up.

Gerry looked at Charles and stopped laughing. "What?"

The noise in the pub grew louder.

"I've heard a rumour. You didn't hear this from me, right?"

"Right," said Gerry hesitantly...

Gerry didn't know how to take the information relayed to him by Charles and sat back in his chair. He felt as if a meat grinder was attacking his brain, but he didn't realise things were about to get a lot worse. Charles gave him a reassuring smile, similar to a doctor who's just informed a patient that he only had days to live.

Gerry stood up and went out into the street side and leant on the black railings. He held onto the railings with one hand when he smelt a fragrance. He thought it to be flowers from the garden, but then realised it smelt more like a perfume. At that point it dawned on him that it wasn't just any perfume, but that of someone he knew. Nastya!

***

A new gear!

Lisa called Paul Timmingham - a pre-arranged call.

"Where are you?" asked Paul.

"Montenegro. How's things?

"You sure get around; I thought you were in Thailand?"

"Too dangerous. There's a mafia guy there called P. Bun Ma who's somehow involved, and he's getting very active. I tried to get into Gerry's house but later decided that it would've been a suicide mission."

"Gerry's back in England by the way."

"Really?"

"I've, shall we say, put a spanner in the works."

"Do tell," said Lisa.

"Well, I don't know if you know, but he has a buddy called Charles Vere in the house. So I've decided to liven things up."

"This sounds epic, what *have* you done?"

"I got a word to Charles about a rape. I've got the source to imply that Gerry is involved. If gossip chains follow their course, Charles should have told Gerry by now. He would be suspended from Parliament during the enquiry and that would make him a liability to Reklem and co. You can imagine the consequences."

"Who's the 'victim'?"

"A girl in Koh Samui, so there's no real comeback. She's going to go on TV with an altered voice and shadowed face."

"I think I know what you're doing here... you're trying to get P. Bun Ma into Gerry's mind. Gerry could conceive this to be a plot to oust him."

"Spot on smarty-pants, the thing is his line of enquiry will be completely in the wrong direction. By thousands of miles. Literally."

"I can add to this Paul," and Lisa paused.

"How so?" asked Paul, now intrigued.

"I can get into, or someone I know, can get into, Five Palms House."

"I got you. Who though?"

"Detective Gunn."

"Who?"

"He's someone Julian ran into years ago. He works out of Nathon police station. It's a huge coincidence so don't ask. Can you check him out? See if he's on P. Bun Ma's payroll."

"I think I can do that. Let me get back to you."

"The iron's hot," said Lisa, "anything else to report?"

"Isn't that enough?" scoffed Paul, "Oh, actually yes, you saw that the chancellor, dear Mr Brun, sold the gold?"

"At a reduced rate thanks to the early announcement. P. Panya and his motley crew must be happy."

"I'm sure they are. Anyway, we'll stop this soon, hopefully," said Paul. "I take it you're sniffing around Reklem as you're on her turf now?"

"I am. She's changed her appearance so she's hard to identify. I don't think she knows what I look like either. Actually, it's why I scarpered from Samui. Gerry, I presume, knows what I look like. It was a tricky situation and P. Bun Ma wanders around like an alpha lion in a pride."

"Be careful Lisa... talk soon."

"Likewise." Lisa hung up and stared in thought at the phone. She realised things had moved up a gear and it was close to *all or nothing* time.

***

Attack

Gerry woke up in his flat and was now living in a nightmare. His head hurt from the alcohol, but he was focused as he knew he had to be. The *chain of greed* was about to expel him (the link of *revenge*), providing what Charles told him was true. Gerry now presumed they considered him to be the weakest link – a link which had a key. No one knew the key was missing, so perhaps the 'team' was trying to get it, thinking he still had it. He considered if Charles was telling the truth or if this was some sort of plan to shake his tree and make him do something stupid.

Reluctantly, he went back to the thought of Nastya's perfume. It wasn't his imagination as there were no girls around when he smelt it. He seemed to be under attack on all fronts and still he had no allies. He did have one ace, which he considered a BIG one. Ten million in the bank!

He decided to prioritise on moving it around so no one could get hold of it. He stopped everything and rang the bank.

Knowing his recent luck and run of events, Gerry wondered if his bank account had been frozen as he dialled out.

"...that's no problem, is there anything else I can do Mr Absalom?" concluded the bank manager.

"No that's fine, thank you," and Gerry put the phone down. Various offshore accounts would have a million pounds deposited by midday that day.

With the decks cleared, he could now refocus with a clearer mind. The rape allegation was foremost in his mind now, and he figured that P. Bun Ma was behind it. Gerry was suspicious of Charles' story. Gerry realised that he would have to terminate P. Bun Ma before he did the same to him. This was, in effect, war! His mind then drifted to those placed in the Cabinet. It could be a simple grudge by an individual he thought, as it dawned on him, that he wasn't all that popular. Perhaps nothing would happen at all, and there would be no rape accusations.

A curtain moved slightly in the living room where he sat working out his options. It moved only momentarily but it was enough for Gerry to see and acknowledge. As no windows were open, he got up and walked slowly to the curtain and stood about half a meter away from it. He put his hand out to touch it, and then moved the curtain to see if anything was behind. There was nothing. He stood a moment longer then returned to his chair and sat down. He wanted to say 'Nastya, is that you?' but dared not for fear of a reply. He watched the curtain for quite a while, but nothing happened. He smelt nothing.

***

Gunn was still at a loss at what to do with Doctor Jah. She couldn't stay hidden forever and she couldn't be brought in as there were eyes and ears everywhere.

"Tam, I've been thinking about Doctor Jah. Do you have any ideas?" he asked across the desk.

"I've been speaking with her of course and she understands, but she seems confused as to why she's a target."

"Beats me too, I'd love to know what's in that deposit box," wondered Gunn out loud, "Whatever it is, I'm sure it's worth a fortune."

"Should we announce that we have the key? That would flush out whoever it is out there, as they would have to come after us and would take Jah off the 'persons of interest' list."

"Not a bad plan Tam, dangerous, but not bad. We could leave a false trail. Send them in the wrong direction. Actually, here's a problem. *Them* includes P. Bun Ma. He's like an anchor, we can't do anything with him in the picture."

Tam looked Gunn in the eyes, "You saying we should get rid of him?"

Gunn didn't respond immediately, which in Tam's eyes meant that it was a consideration. "No," replied Gunn, "don't be silly."

"Let's send Jah back to Koh Ngai. She'll be safe there and no one will find her. We can put out a story that she had to visit a sick relative in Chang Mai, or something," interjected Tam.

"We could also pretend she's somewhere here and see who comes out of the woodwork. Interesting. Tam my man, we have a plan." Gunn raised his eyebrows at the rhyme, and Tam grinned.

* * *

Time for a change

The Italian gold had been relocated to Tivat, Montenegro via Bari, Italy, and the plan was finally reaping rewards for the perpetrators. The treacherous political guardians of the gold were remaining silent as they were too busy counting their rewards. Charles and Gerry, amongst others, were now getting seriously rich and more millions were pouring into their accounts.

Gerry was the first to realise that the richer the participants got, the more unstable became the *chain*. People he understood, can never have enough when they are *so* devious. Someone somewhere will always want more, whether it be power or money, criminals operating in harmony seldom happens. Like it or not, considered Gerry, the team had to be thinned down to keep on top of it. The upper echelon of the group needed to be reduced, as he knew you couldn't have several emperors. There needs to be one ruler so Gerry would have to take down the real leader. P. Panya. He was the political side of things backed by the East.

Because of this, P. Panya had a lot of power, so it would take a monumental event to bring him down. Gerry started to think about someone else within the chain to be incriminated should the deed be done. One name sprung to mind immediately, that of Reklem who P. Panya visited regularly. She could be deemed to have a motive considering the circumstances. Gerry realised a seed had been sown.

***

Double shock!

Tam was just getting into his car when Gunn realised that he hadn't taken the Siam bank key off him. He ran into the road in front of Tam to stop him from leaving.

"What's up boss?"

"The key," said Gunn, a little out of breath, "The key!"

"Shit, yes, sorry!" and Tam pulled out the key from the glove compartment.

Gunn looked at the key in his hand with the Siam Bank tag on it.

"You're joking, right?"

Tam looked up bemused. Gunn could see that Tam wasn't aware of the situation.

"This isn't the key, deposit box keys are different."

Tam turned off the engine, "But it's what Jah gave to me."

They looked at each other in realisation, "Oh no!" said Gunn.

Upon their shared realisation, they immediately drove the thirty minutes to the Beach Republic resort and the bungalows that sat behind it. She was gone!

"Oh no, no, no, NO!" moaned Gunn in despair. He was back to square one. They stood a while in silence and looked at the sea, unsure of what to do next.

"I have no idea what's going on," said Gunn, breaking the silence. "She can't be involved, can she?"

"Dunno boss."

Gunn couldn't put out a search for Doctor Jah as he didn't know who was on his side.

"This is mental," said Gunn, kicking a can into the long grass then realising the irony of this action. "Well, she's gone. Better get back."

They acted as if nothing had happened when they returned to the station. Gunn got the photo albums out for something to do whilst checking his messages. He aimlessly started flicking through them, revisiting the ones with Doctor Jah and Sawa, searching for something he may have missed. In doing so, he noticed something that he wasn't looking for before. "Who's she I wonder?"

"Who?" asked Tam.

"Her," and Gunn pointed to a third girl who appeared in the photos. Actually, she was in all the photos with the two girls. Gunn looked carefully. The girl had a gap in her front teeth. She was quite distinguishable. Gunn sat back and rolled his eyes. "Follow me Tam, and don't say a word."

Tam obeyed. When they got outside, they got straight in the car.

"So?" asked Tam.

"Siam Bank, now! The receptionist has a gap in her teeth. THIS gap!" and Gunn pointed to the girl's teeth in the photos.

"Oh, shit!" said Tam.

At the Bophut Junction of Gunn's 'road' there were a lot of police cars all flashing their lights. Policemen were waving at cars to stop. Tam stopped. Two policemen came up the road to the car. Tam lowered the window.

"Who are you?" asked one policeman with his hand on his gun.

"Gunn, Detective Gunn. I'm police."

The reaction from the police officer was not what they expected.

The policeman pulled out his gun and pointed it at Gunn.

"Out of the car, NOW!" he shouted.

Both officers had by now drawn their guns, and Tam and Gunn were told to kneel in front of the car before they were searched.

"What's going on?" asked Gunn calmly.

"You're under arrest for the murder of P. Bun Ma."

Tam looked at Gunn - speechless.

Part 2

to follow...

To Kseniya, Daniel, Boo & Lapki

Special thanks to Elizabeth Fowkes for helping me format the book

Printed in Great Britain
by Amazon

48884911R00149